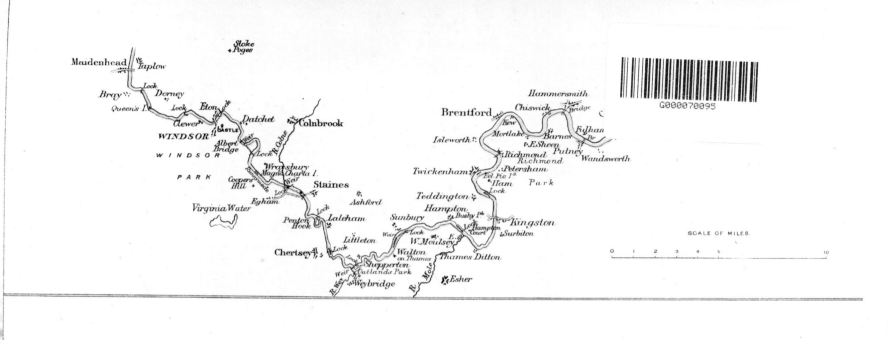

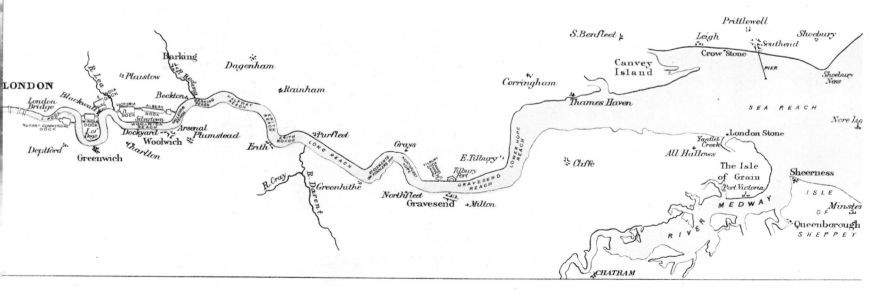

The

VICTORIAN THAMES

Sunbury Lock

The VICTORIAN THAMES

D.G. WILSON

Oxfordshire Books

ALAN SUTTON

First published in the United Kingdom in 1993
Alan Sutton Publishing Ltd
Phoenix Mill • Far Thrupp • Stroud • Gloucestershire

Oxfordshire Books • Oxfordshire County Council Leisure and Arts • Central Library • Westgate • Oxford

First published in the United States of America in 1993
Alan Sutton Publishing Inc
83 Washington Street • Dover • NH 03820

British Library Cataloguing in Publication Data
Wilson, David Gordon
Victorian Thames
I. Title
942.2081

ISBN 0–7509–0183–7

Library of Congress Cataloging in Publication Data applied for

Jacket Illustration: The Lock *by Hector Cafffieri RI, RBA, depicting Cookham Lock on the River Thames (photograph by courtesy of Richard Hagen Limited, Broadway)*
Endpapers: Reproduced from The Thames from its rise to the Nore *by Walter Armstrong, 1889*

Typeset in 11/14 Bembo.
Typesetting and origination by
Alan Sutton Publishing Limited.
Printed in Great Britain by
The Bath Press, Avon.

Contents

Henley Bridge on Regatta Day

Introduction

The River Thames rises in the Cotswolds and meanders gently eastwards, across a wide, open flood plain towards Oxford, flanked, as it is for much of its journey, by mile upon mile of fertile gravel terraces laid down during past ice ages. On its way it collects waters from tributaries draining a vast area of water-bearing limestone uplands, without which the river could never have served man so well over thousands of years as a dependable trade route and source of water, food and power. At Oxford, swelled by the River Cherwell, it turns south; at Goring it breaks through the great chalk limestone ridge that crosses southern England, leaving the Berkshire Downs to the west and the Chilterns to the east. Bearing eastwards again towards Reading, it gathers up the River Kennet and meanders its way through the Middle Thames Valley, until it is turned southwards by the magnificent chalk escarpment of Cliveden and Taplow. Now almost fully grown, the Thames rambles across the open landscape of the London Basin, to at last meet tidal waters at Teddington, 146½ miles (236 km) from its source. Here begins the Londoners' river, brown with silt from far-away fields, surging to and fro with the tide past the nation's capital. There are still another 68½ miles (110 km) before the Nore, a particular shoal off the Isle of Grain, is reached, where officially the river becomes the sea.

For centuries the Thames saw comparatively little change in the craft that plied its inland waters. Great commercial sailing barges, often towed by gangs of men or horse teams, carried

The River Thames above Oxford

essential supplies into the heart of southern England, returning downstream with agricultural products to feed the ever-growing population of London. At the end of the eighteenth century, products of the Industrial Revolution were carried along the Thames through the newly opened connecting waterways, such as the Thames and Severn, and Oxford canals. The slightly later

Grand Junction Canal, which joined the tidal river at Brentford, and the Kennet and Avon Canal, linking Bristol with Reading, also helped for a time to boost the Thames trade.

Numerous Acts of Parliament had been passed to improve navigation on the river which was then administered by the Thames Commissioners. They constructed pound locks to replace the ancient system of passing craft through mill dams and fish weirs by means of flash locks. However, the rapid expansion of the railway network by the middle of the nineteenth century brought a dramatic decline in waterborne commerce and in the tolls which financed river maintenance. Stretches of the river, particularly upstream of Oxford, were virtually abandoned and reverted to nature as locks and weirs fell into disrepair.

The story of the Thames during the Victorian period cannot be told without commenting on the subject of sewage. Early in the nineteenth century many towns had installed main drainage systems to replace traditional earth closets. However, the drain outlets invariably led straight to the nearest river. A river such as the Thames could naturally re-process and render harmless most of the substances the human race poured into it, but a rapidly growing urbanized population together with industrialization was soon to lead to horrific pollution, particularly on the tidal Thames in the vicinity of London. Thames-side towns took much of their water supply from the river or nearby bore-holes. London drew ever-increasing supplies from further upstream near Hampton, Middlesex, from the Metropolitan Water Company intakes.

The first half of the nineteenth century brought major outbreaks of disease to many places, particularly to the capital, where thousands died of cholera. The disease was still endemic in Reading in 1867. The general ambience of the Thames near London at the time was vividly described in an early OARSMAN'S GUIDE, quoted by Mr and Mrs S.C. Hall in their BOOK OF THE THAMES in 1859.

The enormous traffic of London, its increased dirt, and even its increased and statutory habits of cleanliness, its sewage, coal-smoke and coal-gas, tiers of barges, and steamboat piers, have done their work; but not so the Corporation of London, ancient conservators of the *status quo* of a river, noble in spite of its debasement: not so the Crown, or, worse than all, the population of London, and we may say, the nation itself. The lunging surf of the river steamers stirs from its oozy bed, in the rear of some friendly obstruction, the sleepy sediment of the tainted Thames. A ceaseless passage of steam-craft ploughs through the sludgy compromise between

The Upper Thames Valley

the animal, the vegetable, and the mineral kingdoms. Feeble rays from a clouded sun glimmer through the murky atmosphere, and play with tarnished glister over the dingy flood. Fishes, wiser in their generation than ourselves, have forsaken in disgust a medium which in these latitudes has long since ceased to be a definite element; poisoned by impurities to which their simple natures are utterly averse, and scared by circumstances over which they feel they have no earthly control. Odours that speak aloud stalk over the face of the so-called 'waters'.

In 1857, one of the 'Big Stink' years in London, Parliament began to tackle the problem of water pollution by establishing the first Thames Conservancy Board. This was a body independent of local interests, with an initial mandate to address the pollution problem, and in due course to take under its wing all aspects of river management, such as navigation, fisheries and land drainage. However, at first its limited powers over the local authorities, and a jurisdiction only extending up to Staines, proved inadequate. The death in 1861 of the Queen's Consort, Prince Albert, from typhoid reputedly caused by an infection from the foul drains below Windsor Castle, may have hastened the second Act of 1866, when the Conservancy's powers were increased and extended up to Cricklade, in Wiltshire, enabling it to begin pollution control above the capital's water intakes.

The Conservancy immediately served notices on the Thames-side local authorities to stop discharging raw sewage directly into the river. Some were quickly persuaded and within a few years constructed sewage treatment plants. But the larger towns such as Windsor, Reading, Abingdon and Oxford, where the problems were greatest and the remedy more costly, took longer. Oxford did not have a treatment works until 1880. Even the river upstream of Oxford continued to be polluted by towns

such as Cricklade until at least 1895, although in 1875 H.R. Robertson in LIFE ON THE UPPER THAMES stated that the clearness of the water was at times quite startling, and in the absence of a well or pump the poorer classes drew drinking water straight from the river, apparently with few harmful effects.

From 1880, Londoners could expect comparatively safe water from the Thames at Hampton. However, below there towards the tidal river, many districts still discharged untreated waste for another decade or more. Sir Joseph Bazalgette, best known for the construction of the Victoria Embankment in London, was the brilliant engineer who had designed the vast trunk sewer system which took the waste of the capital further downstream nearer the estuary, to be discharged at Barking and Crossness. Treatment works were eventually established here and solid

Dredging at Abingdon

waste dumped out at sea. Many other improvements followed, and by the end of the Victorian Age through vast expenditure, inventiveness and dedication, the Londoners' Thames had been revived. Although no stately salmon could yet run up with the tide, as in previous centuries, by 1902 it was worthwhile for at least two professional fishermen to work the tideway at Chiswick.

The Thames Conservancy was also created to provide an independent navigation authority responsible for improvements to the Port of London, such as dredging the seaward deep water channels, repairing sea-walls and regulating the increasing steam-boat traffic and passenger landing stages. In 1866, it took over the Upper Navigation from Staines to Cricklade from the near-bankrupt Thames Navigation Commissioners. Commercial traffic on the non-tidal river had already drastically declined following the establishment of the first stages of the railway network and with insufficient income for maintenance, many locks and weirs had become derelict and dangerous to use. The Conservancy had a meagre income from the Public Works Loan Commissioners and merchandise tolls, later augmented by contributions from abstraction by the water companies. In the first few years it somehow made a large number of improvements to locks, weirs and towing-paths throughout the length of the river. It implemented by-laws, through Acts of Parliament, to regulate commercial fishing and angling, the shooting of wild life, the speed and safety of steam launches and later electric and petrol-driven craft. In 1909 it relinquished control of the tidal river to the Port of London Authority and concentrated its efforts on the 136 miles (219 km) of river between Teddington Lock and Cricklade.

The responsibilities and expertise of the Thames Conservancy increased as Man made increasing demands on the once comparatively unspoilt natural river for recreation, water abstraction, land drainage and also flood prevention, the latter made necessary as he perversely continued to build on the flood plain. A century later it was able to hand over to the subsequent technocratic and commercial organizations one of the most intensively used but best-managed waterways on earth.

The nineteenth-century navigational improvements came too late to slow the decline of commercial traffic on the upper reaches, but they were just in time for the Victorians' sudden passion for pleasure boats and rowing. Professional watermen had been plying the Thames for centuries in many types of rowed craft, from passenger wherries to huge ceremonial barges, and raced for prizes such as the Doggett's Coat and Badge, which dates from 1715. But the first amateur recreational and competitive rowing seems to have been initiated at Eton and Oxford in the 1790s. Eight-oared craft were raced at Oxford from 1815; the first Oxford versus Cambridge University race taking place at Henley in 1829. The single scull competition 'between gentlemen', for the Wingfield Sculls, dates from 1830. As the condition of the Thames improved, rowing became a fashionable recreational and social pastime. Boat builders adapted the lines of traditional wherries to construct single and double skiffs, gigs, randans and the like, which in their hundreds became the work-horses of the Victorian boating era.

The boom could not have happened without the new railway system, which for the first time gave Londoners a cheap form of transport to escape for a few days from the cramped living and working conditions which pervaded the capital. Brunel's Great Western Railway had reached the Thames-side towns of Maidenhead and Reading, the villages of Pangbourne, Goring and Moulsford by 1840, and Oxford four years later. Branches soon followed to other fashionable boating centres: to Windsor in 1849, Bourne End by 1854, with a private extension to Great Marlow in 1868. The Twyford to Henley branch was opened in 1857.

Pleasure-boating at Twickenham

As England prospered, large sections of the population were able to afford the time and money for leisure activities, and from the 1870s thousands began to flock to the river in the summer months to participate in pleasure-boating. Ancient riverside inns and boat yards, built originally for the barge trade, were quickly adapted to cater for the new trend, while throughout the Thames Valley suburban villas and bungalows, built as country retreats and commuter homes, colonized villages which had been comparatively isolated before the coming of the railway. American novelist Henry James was fascinated by the strange habits of the English race, and published articles for American readers. These were later produced in book form as ENGLISH

HOURS, illustrated by Joseph Pennell. In one article, first published in 1888, James neatly encapsulates the extent of the Thames pleasure-boating craze.

From Westminster to the sea its uses are commercial, but none the less pictorial for that; while in the other direction – taking it properly a little further up – they are personal, social, athletic, idyllic. In its recreative character it is absolutely unique. I know of no other classic stream that is so splashed about for the mere fun of it. There is something almost droll and at the same time touching in the way that on the smallest pretext of holiday or fine weather the mighty population takes to the boats. They bump each other in the narrow, charming channel, between Oxford and Richmond they make an uninterrupted procession. Nothing is more suggestive of the personal energy of the people and their eagerness to take, in the way of exercise and adventure, whatever they can get. I hasten to add that what they get on the Thames is exquisite, in spite of the smallness of the scale and the contrast between the numbers and space. In a word, if the river is the busiest suburb of London it is also by far the prettiest. That term applies to it less, of course, from the bridges down, but it is only because in this part of its career it deserves a larger praise.

Many publications were produced for the Victorian boating fraternity, most being narratives of river journeys, describing scenery and giving potted histories of riverside churches, mansions, villages and towns, sometimes noting the facilities that were provided. One of the first was THE ROWING ALMANACK AND OARSMAN'S COMPANION of 1862, by 'W.H.R.', which contained such items as the results of events, lists of past champions, and a distance table naming every lock, weir and bridge from Inglesham (just above Lechlade) to

London Bridge. The full list of weirs or flash locks above Oxford is unusual as at the time that part of the river was said to be almost unnavigable. Some books and guides simply start the downstream journey at Oxford.

Advertisements within the *Almanack* illustrate the early exploitation of the river for leisure. Bankside inns offered accommodation for the oarsmen, angler and artist, with incentives such as 'Particular attention paid to the sleeping and culinary departments'. The Iron Steam Boat Company and City Steam Boat Company (Limited), advertised Tideway services as frequently as every five, ten and fifteen minutes from the City to various piers up to Chelsea and Kew.

John and Stephen Salter up at Oxford advertised that they built, sold and hired 'Eight, Four, Pair-oared and Sculling Outriggers, Gigs, Funnies, Canoes, Large and Small Skiffs, Pleasure Boats, Punts and Dinghies, suitable for Lakes and Ornamental Water, Yachts and centre-board Sailing Boats, Oars, Sculls, Sails, Cushions, &c.' Second-hand Eights could be purchased for £6. Rowing boats were let for excursions from Oxford to London, with charges from £5. 10s. 0d. (£5.50) for an Eight-oar, to a sculling gig at £1. 10s. 0d. (£1.50) Salter's had a boat house at the Feathers Tavern, Wandsworth, whence craft were brought back to Oxford by horse-drawn van at no extra charge.

Under the 1885 Act, the Conservancy laid down by-laws for the protection of Thames fisheries and prohibited public shooting over or near the river. This did not affect existing fowling, hunting and sporting rights of riparian land owners. The few otters that were left were still being persecuted in 1905, when a Chief Inspector's order was issued to lock and weir keepers in the Oxford area, warning them against killing or trapping them.

It seems that not only wildlife but the human riverside population was also threatened. A.J. Church wrote in ISIS AND THAMESIS in 1886 as follows:

In my own boyhood and youth I spent much time upon the river, and I can recall days when the solitude so dear to an angler – and it was as an angler that I haunted the most 'fishy' of English rivers – was rarely broken by a passing boat. Two or three pleasure-boats, as may fishing-punts, and perhaps twice as many barges, would be all that would pass between sunrise and sunset. (It will be understood that I speak of those reaches of the river that are not in the immediate neighbourhood of towns.)

It is hardly necessary to say how much all this has changed. The barges are scarcely more frequent than they were; in some sections of the river they are, I fancy, less so. But a pleasure traffic, that is nothing less than vast, has sprung up; a continuous stream – on Bank holidays it may also be said a positive torrent – of boats, and, *infandum dictu*, of steam-launches, passes up and down the river. And here I would say a word, by the way, in defence of these much-abused persons, the riparian proprietors. It is not to be wondered at, when we compare what the Thames was and what it is, that they assert and seek to enforce the rights of private ownership over backwaters and islands. They once lived in seclusion, and they now find themselves in the blaze of publicity; they feel as the dweller in some remote farmhouse might be supposed to feel if he found his home suddenly transported to Piccadilly. Their privacy is invaded by an army which, not without some of the unpleasing features of military occupation, bivouacs on their lawns and erects posts of observation opposite to their dining-room windows.

The technique of 'camping out', by which, at the end of a day's row, one either slept in the boat under a canvas cover, or in a tent set up on the bank, developed in the 1870s. It was encouraged by the example set by enthusiasts such as Henry

Goring and Streatley Regatta

Taunt of Oxford, who, in his classic guidebook A NEW MAP OF THE THAMES, described its advantages for the City man as an escape to pure country air from his labours at a desk in London's foul atmosphere. It also had the advantage of being a cheap alternative to hotel or guest-house accommodation, which in the season could be sometimes impossible to obtain unless one had booked in advance. One need not have to 'rough it' to any great degree – successful men like Taunt took along their 'man' to do the fetching and carrying, and perhaps much of the rowing. But the example of a party seen by Charles Dickens Junior at Cookham, with a servant in livery laying the table for dinner, was, he says, not to be followed.

A lucrative service industry soon developed, to supply not only boats, but items such as tents and waterproof canvas, boating dress for both sexes, wicker hampers, eating and cooking utensils, folding beds and hammocks, and, of course, provisions, particularly potted and tinned foods. Two essential items were a tin opener, the lack of which led to an hilarious episode with a tin of pineapple portrayed by Jerome in THREE MEN IN A BOAT, and a hatchet for chopping wood for fuel. Taunt recommends that wood should be purchased at a wheelwright's or carpenter's shop, but it seems that too often people obtained free wood by indiscriminate cutting on private land. Dickens cites the case of an estate owner who had allowed camping, only to be repaid by the destruction of valuable shrubs and the theft of farm produce.

Landowners understandably objected to trespassing and vandalism on property which contained valuable trees, crops and livestock. Jerome, a townee, rails at the private notices on the banks and arrogantly dismisses the rights of landowners, seemingly unaware that most land is privately owned or leased, holding the same rights as a suburban garden.

Riverside residents also had to contend with a growing number of box-like houseboats from the 1870s onwards. In the summer months the houseboats were towed up the river and moored in the best scenic spots, but convenient to the railway. Many in private ownership were of enormous size and opulence, while others, of a more humble nature, were hired out for the season. As numbers escalated, the Conservancy designated special mooring areas for houseboats and in 1894, when there were 160 or so in use, a by-law forbade the disposal of sewage and refuse straight into the river. George D. Leslie R.A., artist, writer and punting expert, had his tongue firmly in his cheek when he discussed houseboats in OUR RIVER (1881).

In all my river experiences I have never tried one of these boats, but they have their charms, no doubt, and much fine, independent pleasure may be got out of them. They look inviting and snug with their little windows and curtains, their bird cages and pots of flowers, the smoke curling up from the kitchen chimney and the cooking and washing-up going on inside; but I cannot help thinking it must be a little tedious, and I have observed, that if not employed on some active business, such as cleaning or cooking, the occupants very often wear rather a blasé expression. There is rather a significant thing about these boats, which is, that after one year's trial they are frequently abandoned, great numbers being often seen at anchor quite tenantless.

Of course, there are house-boats and house-boats. Some of the great saloon barges, varnished and gilt, and furnished with profuse magnificence, refrigerators, pianos, &c., with kitchen in a separate boat and a host of attendant servants, appear sadly out of place on the river, and make one suspect that the proprietors are gentlemen with a penchant for yachting, but deterred from the marine indulgence of their hobby by dread of sea-sickness. In a moderate-sized houseboat an artist or any one fond of the river ought to be pretty happy, especially if he is not above doing a lot of things for himself, as it is precisely the novelty of such work which gives the whole charm to this mode of life; and in any case houseboats are in no sense open to the objections of the steam launch.

The industrial expansion and subsequent affluence of the Victorian Age could not have happened without the steam engine, in all its forms, and which at an early stage was used as propulsion for boats. The first experimental passenger-carrying paddle steamers appeared on the tidal Thames in about 1814. In spite of the occasional exploding boiler their popularity grew, and within a decade fleets of excursion and ferry boats were churning the waters from the estuary to Richmond. Wide paddle boxes on either side of such boats prevented them from passing up through the locks. However, the invention of screw or propeller drive for steam launches which now could be built with narrower beam, enabled them to use the upper river. Writers of the time, who had only known the tranquil silence of a river whose craft were only towed, rowed, paddled, sailed or punted, were unanimous in their condemnation of these brash intruders. C.H. Cook in THAMES RIGHTS AND WRONGS, wrote that in 1870 there were only six of 'these pests', but by 1895, the year his book was published, there were about four hundred. He bemoans the fact that the Thames Conservancy did not have the powers to impose a limit on the number or size of craft, or control their design to lessen the wash which caused damage to banks, aquatic growth and small craft.

By modern standards the wash caused by displacement-hulled steam launches is not great, except at high speed. Nevertheless, many today would wish those powers could have been obtained at the time, in order to regulate the far worse scourge of modern craft more suited to the sea than inland waters.

Camping out

George Leslie's musings on the steam launches in OUR RIVER are probably of little consequence to the majority who have only known a motorized means of transport. Nevertheless, they are just as valid today as they were in 1881.

The much vexed question as to the use and abuse of steam launches on the river would, from its importance, require a whole chapter to itself; but as I am perfectly hostile to the launches, and it may be, slightly prejudiced in the matter, there would not be much use in my attempting to discuss the subject in an argumentative manner. I would, therefore, rather class the launches amongst those things which, in my opinion, are simply mistakes. I do not believe it is possible to really appreciate the river from on board a launch. The motion of the boat causes the perspective, both in front and behind, to alter so rapidly in a converging and diverging manner, as to have on the eye quite a painful effect, which after a short time becomes very wearisome. In the bows the wind and spray render a steady gaze a-head very uncomfortable, and a smoke out of the question. In this part of the vessel the passengers generally sit, as depicted in Walker's inimitable drawing in *Punch*, with their backs to the view. In the stern the view is spoilt by the launch's smoke and swell, the banks are washed by a travelling wave, and the pretty floating weeds are all in wild commotion. Here too, all is gritty and black from the smoke stack, and the odious smell of the rancid engine oil is anything but the attar of roses.

Inside the cabin the air is close and confined to a degree. No part of the boat is free from the everlasting jig-jigging vibration from the screw, which will produce an almost certain headache to a novice in steamboat travelling.

What I really believe the misguided owners enjoy, and the only thing, is themselves: it is the feeling of pride that delights – the pride of being seen as the captain of a private yacht adorned with brass nobs and polished fittings, brass-banded water-casks, gilding, monograms, flags, etc.; to go puffing along with a stoker and boy under your command; the pleasure of whistling to announce yourself to the lock-keepers, or to warn boats in front; to have an excuse for wearing the manly flannels of the rowing man, without exercising a single muscle in them: these are the main temptations that usually induce people to set up a launch.

After each season's use of the boat an increase in the size of its owner is likely to take place, but not exactly in the arms, shoulders or legs. An appetite will no doubt come from merely being in the open air, but the healthy perspiration is wanting, and the ease with which drinks of all kinds can be consumed on board, especially as there is little else to do, has a direct tendency to corpulence and enlarged liver.

I am fond of studying the looks of people on board these boats, and from repeated observations I am quite sure they seldom feel happy on their voyages. They are generally rather pompous, and laugh and talk to one another, but the wholesome happiness which proceeds from labour is entirely absent. There is no pleasure in arriving anywhere in a launch like that of landing from a small boat which you have navigated yourself. . . .

I have so seldom travelled in these boats, and when I have it has been under such exceptionally favourable conditions, that I daresay I am unaware of a great many other drawbacks and unpleasantnesses incurred by their proprietors. The cost of the craft when new, the trouble of looking after it and the constant something wanting to be done to the engine, the bore of employing men and stokers, the supplies of coal that have repeatedly to be obtained, the engine-fitter's bills for repairs, and a variety of other petty annoyances, such as breaking down on a journey, or running aground, must form some slight set-off to the transient joy of dashing along for twenty miles once or twice during the summer, in all the glory of steamboat proprietorship. I confess to having witnessed, once or twice, with great pleasure the discomfiture of a disabled launch, the lump of a boat being towed downstream to the nearest large town, on account of a broken shaft, or something wrong with its injector, or else stuck helplessly aground on a sandbank. Besides which the numbers of faded, dingy-looking, second-hand launches lying here and there, at different places, for sale or hire, gradually getting more and more rusty and dilapidated, tell tales of the rapidity with which their former owners grew tired of them. At Hampton, Surbiton, and Richmond there are a very large number of these abandoned favourites, safely moored, and I am glad to say, eating their boilers off.

Houseboat Stella *at Henley*

My readers will have observed that I have not in these remarks alluded to the well-known objections that have been so often made against the launches on the score of the damage they do. I have passed over the serious injury they cannot help causing to the banks, no matter how slowly they proceed; the heavy curses of the injured fishermen, artists, and boat-letters; the fright of the ladies and nervous people; the frequent accidents, many of a fatal character; the fouling of the water, the smoke, the disturbance, the whistling and general ugliness. . . .

Jerome K. Jerome's way of dealing with steam launches was to drift right into their path, pretending that the launch did not exist, and, with luck, make it go aground. He says, 'I never see a steam launch but I feel I should like to lure it to a lonely part of the river, and there in the silence and the solitude, strangle it.'

Passenger steamer entering Sunbury Lock

Leslie, Jerome and Cook perhaps had more controversial views than other nineteenth-century Thames travellers, most of which seem to have been content to give an anecdotal and descriptive account of their journey down the river. Excursions between Lechlade or Oxford and London were taken in the downstream direction and, therefore, traditionally, with a few exceptions, descriptions of the river have been from source to sea. Most authors concentrated on describing only the features in the surrounding landscape, the beautiful scenery, and the histories of the places they passed. Few give detailed descriptions of the river itself, the locks and weirs, its trades, industries, and the people along its course. In this book, extracts have been gleaned from the most informative works in an effort to re-create the river environment seen through eyes of those earlier travellers on their collective journey from source to sea.

Words are not enough, however. If we are to put flesh on the

Henry Taunt at Wallingford

bones of an account of the Victorian Thames, there was one outstanding artist whose work cannot be ignored, and that is the Oxford photographer Henry Taunt. From the 1860s, his passion for the river led him to take innumerable journeys throughout its length, on his way taking thousands of photographs which are today priceless historical documents. Taunt's photographs have been chosen from the collection in the care of The Oxfordshire Photographic Archive. They recapture the spirit of the Victorian Thames: moments in the lives of ordinary people, working, playing, or just sitting, unchanging village scenes near the source, ancient locks and weirs with their attendant keepers, the channel thronged with punts, skiffs and steam boats at Oxford, fashionable resorts such as Henley and Maidenhead, and scenes of bustling commerce in the Port of London, and on to where the river meets the sea.

Thames Head Meadows and the canal pumping house

CHAPTER ONE

Thames Head to Oxford

The birds, flowers, and bees around are, doubtless, in their several ways, rejoicing with me in the balmy May morning radiant with warm sunshine. Down the unsullied emerald of the little slope yonder, carpeted with nodding cowslips, daisies, and buttercups, and faintly azured in sheltering spaces with wild hyacinths, I have descended into a rustic glade, not, at its widest, more than fifty yards across, and running, roughly reckoning, north and south. The slope is easy, springing as it does from a verdant bottom to the foot of a low wall; pushing aside the glossy sycamore branches, I have leaped from the Canal path, at a gap where the village children, on their recent half-holiday wastefully cast side the surplus of their cowslip harvest to wither and die. But from my present standpoint the low wall is nearly hidden in undergrowth, and by a plentiful intermixture of hawthorn, holly and ash flourishing on the bank top. The sweet-smelling grass is spangled with daisies and buttercups, although not so profusely as in the field adjacent, which is destined for a crop of hay; and the grove resounds with bird-music set in the rapturous key of the bridal season. And there, a few paces athwart the sward, under the shadow of trembling foliage, is the spot which for centuries was said to be the birthplace of the River Thames. We are at Thames Head, in Trewsbury Mead, in the parish of Cotes, in the county of Gloucestershire, three miles south-west of Cirencester.

So begins William Senior's first chapter in THE ROYAL RIVER, a superbly illustrated book, published in 1885, encompassing the Thames from source to sea. The chapters were written by various authors who were each able to concentrate on a limited length of river, resulting in one of the most complete of the many portraits of the Thames and its environs.

Thames Head has been described in a great variety of ways. Most writers appear to have seen it only in summer, when no water may be seen in the tiny channel until one walks for a mile or more across the meadows. In the nineteenth century the lack of water was usually blamed on the pumping from adjacent wells which maintained levels in the Thames and Severn Canal. More recently, artesian wells in the district undoubtedly draw vast quantities from the limestone rocks to feed the town of Swindon in Wiltshire. Nevertheless, substantial rainfall does replenish the water table, allowing even the highest of the ancient springs to burst forth again. A small granite monolith now marks the spot for which some earlier explorers searched in vain.

Over the centuries some have claimed that the true source is at Seven Springs, near Cheltenham, at the head of the River Churn, because its length is greater than that of the main stream when it joins it at Cricklade. Nevertheless, a simple study of the respective catchment areas shows that the Churn has not much more than a single basic stream channel, while the traditional and official Thames Head source sits at the head of a network of streams in a much larger drainage basin.

Less than two miles from Thames Head the infant stream skirts the

The sheep-washing place, Kemble Meadows

village of Kemble. A quiet rural backwater for centuries, it had a rude awakening with the construction on its doorstep of the Cheltenham and Great Western Union Railway, which connected nearby Cirencester to the outside world in 1841. Four years later Kemble itself became an important junction on the main line through the Cotswolds to Gloucester. The coming of this railway put paid to any further hopes of substantial profits on the nearby canal which gradually slipped into decline. The branch railway line to Cirencester has now also passed into history and the stripling Thames trickles through the wide gap in the embankment which once carried the giants of steam.

Before steam there was water power, harnessed on the Thames to drive corn mills, which for a thousand years provided the population

with flour for their daily bread. As we reach Ewen, the next village on our course, Charles Harper in THAMES VALLEY VILLAGES explains that even this close to the source, the Thames had been made to work for man, although by then, at the end of the Victorian period, most rural mills had completed their working lives.

Ewen, standing by the roadside, is remarkable only for its rustic cottages, but they are particularly beautiful in their old unstudied way; heavily thatched, and surrounded with old-fashioned gardens. The Thames begins to flow, or to trickle, regularly at Upper Somerford Mill, whose water-wheel, immense in proportion to the little stream, is picturesquely sheltered under wide-spreading trees. The village of Somerford Keynes lies close at hand. The way between this village and Ashton Keynes passes over rough common land, and enters Ashton Keynes romantically, past the great church, and along a fine avenue of elms beside the manor house, emerging at what, until a few years ago, was Ashton Keynes Mill. . . .

All the old mills that once made the Thames additionally picturesque are disappearing. Some go up in flame and smoke, like Iffley Mill, below Oxford, painted and sketched by a thousand artists, and described by a hundred writers of books and articles, to whose lasting sorrow it was destroyed by fire in 1907. Shiplake Mill met a similar fate a little earlier, and modern milling conditions forbid their ever being rebuilt. Ashton Keynes Mill became disestablished as a mill because it could no longer compete with the modern steam-roller flour mills, that nowadays grind flour much more expeditiously and cheaply than the old water-driven mills. But the old mill house stands, little altered.

Little need be said about Ashton Keynes church, for it is of very late Gothic and plentifully uninteresting, but the village itself is a delight. It is the queen of Upper Thames villages, with a picture at every turn. Here the Thames flows quietly down one side of the village street, and at the beginning of that rural, cottage-bordered, tree-shaded highway is the first bridge across the river; an ancient Gothic bridge, with a slipway beside it, where the horses are brought down to wash their legs in summer. . . .

There are many little bridges spanning the Thames at Ashton Keynes, for the stream washes the old stone garden walls of a long line of cottages, and the entrance to each cottage necessitates a bridge of stone, of brick, or of timber. Stonecrop, candy tuft, wall flowers, arabis, snapdragon, and many other semi-wild plants grow in the crevices of these old walls, and drape them all the summer with an unimaginable mantle of beauty; and where the cottages end, and the highway becomes a straight flat road, making for Cricklade, a modern country residence has been built, with the walls of it going down in the same way into the water, and the wild flowers encouraged in the like fashion to inhabit there. A contemplative person might pass a pleasant time at Ashton Keynes, where there is a homely inn, but none of these unamusing 'amusements' which serve to render places of holiday resort unendurable. For those not very numerous persons who are satisfied with their own company Ashton Keynes affords decided attractions. No one ever goes there, for it is on the road to Nowhere in Particular, and not even the motorcar is a very familiar sight. Thus the ruminative stranger will have his privacy respected; unless indeed he happens to be either an artist or photographer, when he is certain to be surrounded by a dense crowd of children, who seem to become instinctively aware of an open sketchbook or camera at hand, and surround the owners of them in most embarrassing fashion.

Below Ashton Keynes the Thames is joined by the little Swillbrook, and crossed at the confluence by the small, three arched Oaklade Bridge. A mile or so below this Waterhay Bridge, a typical 'county' bridge, whose frame of iron girders and railings, painted white, ill assorts with the luxuriance of swaying reeds and thickly clustered alders that here enshrouds the stream.

Upper Somerford Mill

In the twentieth century Waterhay Bridge has gained the undeserved fame of being claimed as the head of commercial navigation at some unspecified time in the past. The theory can be laid firmly at the door of Henry Taunt who, in his NEW MAP OF THE THAMES (1871), first suggested that seven-ton barges may once have traded there. Unfortunately the usually astute Fred S. Thacker, who, nearly fifty years later, published the 'bible' for all Thames historians, THE THAMES HIGHWAY, follows Taunt, without discovering documentary evidence, and states that here the 'tradition' of serious navigation begins. Others have followed.

The theory can be discounted by referring to seventeenth-century documents quoted by Thacker himself, and to chroniclers such as W. Ireland (1791), S. Westall (1828), and W.G. Fearnside (1834), who all state that the head of navigation was at Cricklade. Here for centuries the river was blocked by the great West Mills, and for a century from

Ashton Keynes

1820, a trifle upstream, by the aqueduct of the North Wilts Canal. Those of us who, when there was sufficient water in the narrow, twisting channel, have paddled and pushed tiny coracle-type boats from Waterhay to Cricklade, would not have wished to try with any sort of barge when, logically, a horse and cart could more easily carry the load the mere two and a half miles by road.

And so to Cricklade, the ancient market town, written of in unflattering terms by some Victorian travellers, but once head of navigation for barges, helped upstream by weirs which deepened the channel from Lechlade. However, as W.G. Fearnside, who wrote the text for Tombleson's illustrated THAMES AND MEDWAY explains, in 1834 it was only navigated by small craft – a situation which remains to this day.

Cricklade Bridge is constructed of brick and stone, and consists of one broad arch. The Thames and Severn Canal passes to the north of the town, and previous to its formation, the first navigation of the river here commenced, barges, carrying from six to seven tons, being freighted with corn, malt, bacon, etc. Since the opening of the canal, all traffic has ceased; and, save the miller's skiff, or fisher's punt, no boat is seen disturbing the peaceful bosom of the gentle Isis. A few yards beyond the bridge, the Churn affords a copious and welcome contribution to the parent stream. This river rises at Cubberley, in Gloucestershire, about ten miles north of Cirencester, and passing through that city joins the Isis at this point. A short distance in advance, the Rey, which commences near Swindon, in Wiltshire, lends also its rivulet force to render the Isis navigable. The river now throws off the languid and sluggish ripple which has hitherto marked its character, and assumes a more active and rapid pace, indicatory of that intense commercial life and bustle, which its waters are eventually engaged in.

Looking upstream to Cricklade

Fearnside's use of the pseudo-classical term 'Isis', meaning the River Thames, will be discussed when we reach the confluence of the little River Thame further downstream.

From 1789 the ten miles of river navigation between Cricklade and Lechlade had been superseded by the Thames and Severn Canal, and apart from the remnants of a few small weirs had lapsed back into its natural state. However, agricultural improvements from the 1860s, especially the extensive use of field drains, induced the Thames Conservancy to combine with the new Thames Valley Drainage Commissioners to improve land drainage. They were soon zealously dredging to deepen ancient stream beds and removing any old structures that might impede river flows.

The Old Bridge, Castle Eaton

Much to the disgust of Thames lovers such as Charles Harper, 'improvements' to open up the channel and obviate flooding became a continuous process. Imagine the shock Harper received when he paid a return visit to Castle Eaton, a village less than four miles down from Cricklade, with an exquisite small church standing above the stream, only to find that the bridge which had completed the scene loved by artists had disappeared.

It is a very quiet village, of a purely agricultural type, and generally littered with straw and fragments of hay. Here the Thames was until quite recent years crossed by a most delightful old bridge, that looked like the ruins of some very ancient structure whose arches had been broken down and the remaining piers crossed by a makeshift affair of white-painted timber. 'Makeshift' is perhaps hardly the word to be properly used here, for it seems to indicate a temporary contrivance; and

The Thames at Kempsford

bridge was all that has just been described – and more; for no pen may write, nor tongue tell, of the beauty of that old, time-worn yet not decrepit bridge, that carried across the Thames a road of no great traffic, and would have continued still safely to carry it for an indefinite period. It was one of the expected delights of revisiting the Upper Thames, to renew acquaintance with this bridge, sketched years before; and it was with a bitter but unavailing regret and a futile anger that, coming to the well-remembered spot, it was seen to have been wantonly demolished, and its place taken by a hideous, low-pitched iron girder bridge, worthy only of a railway company; and so little likely to be permanent that it is observed to be already breaking into rusty scales and scabs beneath its hideous red paint. The ancient elms that once formed a gracious background to the old bridge stand as of old beside the river bank; but the old bridge itself lies, a heap of stones that the destroyers were too lazy to remove, close by, on the spot on which they were first flung. No description, it has been said, can hope to convey the beauty of Castle Eaton Bridge, for the old stone piers were hung with wild growths, and spangled and stained with mosses and lichens. A sketch of one end of it may serve but it once formed the subject of a painting by Ernest Waterlow, and in that medium at least, its hoary charm has been preserved. Let a photograph of its existing successor be here the all-too-shameful evidence of the wicked ways of the Thames Conservancy with this once delightful spot in particular, and with such spots in general. We cannot frame to use language too strong for a crime so heinous against the picturesque.

Let us recapitulate the facts and draw the indictment more exactly against that sinning body. We shall thus ventilate a righteous indignation, and help to create a healthy public feeling against all such damnable doings, by whomsoever done. We are, of necessity, in this country of change and of an

this bridge, if not designed in keeping with the huge, sturdy, shapeless stone and rubble piers, was at any rate sufficiently substantial to have existed for many generations, and to have lasted for many yet to come. Alas that we should have to write of all this in the past tense! But it is so. Twenty years ago, when the present writer paid his first visit to Castle Eaton, the old

Inglesham Lock and the Round House

increasing population, faced with a continuous defacement of places ancient, beautiful and historic; and it behoves us to use our utmost efforts to preserve what we have left. What, then, shall we say of such absolutely unnecessary outrages as this? Shall we not revile the whole body responsible, from the Board and the Secretary down to the chief engineer and the staff of underlings who did the deed? The Thames Conservancy, in fact, has been a most diligent destroyer of the beauty of the river; slaving early and late and overtime in that devil's work, but remaining supremely idle where the encroachments of private persons, or the uglifications by waterworks companies, and modern mill- and factory-builders are concerned. It is the Thames Conservancy that has repaired the banks of the river

and has reinforced the walls of its weirs and lock-cuts, with hideous bags and barrels of concrete, that retain their bag-and-barrel shape for all time, and so render miles of riverside sordid in the extreme. We simply cannot afford these ways with the river.

The line of the now derelict Thames and Severn Canal ran very close to the river at Kempsford, separated from it by the magnificent church, with its square tower prominent in the flat landscape. The Victorian villagers were kept in touch with the outside world by the occasional barge or narrow boat that tied up to the wharf, or by the carrier's horse van that trundled down from Fairford or Lechlade railway stations. The river, low and rich with life in summer or bank full and brown with winter flood, was only disturbed by the fisherman setting eel traps, or an intrepid canoeist coming down with the current from Cricklade.

The ford at Kempsford is very ancient. The area abounds with prehistoric sites, and when the ford was dredged away Saxon weapons were found, lost in a border skirmish that was recorded in the ANGLO-SAXON CHRONICLE. *Thames books tell conflicting histories of the mansion, and the 'Gunners' Room', a mullioned window of which overlooks the river. Perhaps Fearnside's account, part of which follows, is the least fanciful.*

The manor was, in the reign of Edward the Confessor, the property of Earl Harold, but was afterwards granted by the Conqueror to Hernulf de Heseling, a Norman soldier, who had accompanied him to England. After some years it came, by marriage, into the possession of Henry, Earl of Lancaster; and his son, Henry, Duke of Lancaster, occupied here an extensive mansion . . . The Manor ultimately devolved to the Coleraine family, by whose orders the Mansion was levelled with the ground, towards the close of the last century, and the materials purchased by Mr Loveden, of Buscot Park, near Lechlade, who

Lechlade from Inglesham

used them in the structure of the present elegant house belonging to that family. The outer walls, by the side of the river, as well as the entrance porch and gateway, are yet standing, and also the stabling and out-houses, which are used for farming purposes and a dwelling.

The summer river at Kempsford is relatively deep and slow, but, still within sight of the church tower, the winding stream suddenly narrows, *and slides beneath Hannington Bridge. After the removal of Ham Weir, below the bridge, and Inglesham Weir in about 1865, the next three miles to Inglesham could, and still can be, very shallow in places. Near Inglesham, however, the Thames is joined by the River Cole from the edge of the chalk downland to the south, and the Coln from the Cotswolds in the north. Within a mile or so comes the confluence of the River Leach, which gave its name to nearby Lechlade. Together the waters combine to make the channel deep and wide enough for large commercial barges; consequently Inglesham became the logical point for the canal from beyond the Cotswolds to join the river. The confluence is marked by Inglesham Lock and its 'Round House', a circular, two-storied lock cottage.*

The heyday of the canals had come and gone when Mr and Mrs S.C. Hall came researching for THE BOOK OF THE THAMES, published in 1859. They paint a depressing picture of the decline of commercial navigation, not knowing of course, that the new Conservancy would soon be trying to revitalize the Upper Thames and that eventually, in the coming age of affluence, tourists would replace the bargemen.

We have now arrived at that point in the Thames where it becomes navigable for boats of burthen; the canal conveys in barges, each from thirty to sixty tons, the produce of the four quarters of the globe into several parts of England; the port of Bristol is thus united with that of London; other canals are combined with this: and so an internal communication was formed, the value of which may be readily estimated before the introduction of steam. But the railways have placed this mode of traffic almost in abeyance – the canals are comparatively idle, and ere long, perhaps, will be altogether deserted. The passage of a boat through the lock is now an event of rare occurrence: it is seldom opened more than once or twice in a week. Greater speed is obtained by the railway, of course, but the chief impediment arises from the cost incurred in passing through the locks and weirs along the Thames. These 'costs' may have been much reduced – probably are so – but they continue greatly to impede 'traffic'. The natural consequence is, that steam absorbs all the traffic, except to places remote from stations; and that boats are in use only for heavy cargoes, chiefly timber and coal. The towing-paths between Lechlade and Oxford, in consequence of the causes we have observed upon, are so little

disturbed as to be scarcely perceptible: they are for the most part so 'grass o'ergrown' as to be distinguished from the meadow only after a careful search. Indeed, all along the Thames bank to Lechlade, and much lower, almost until we approach Oxford, there is everywhere a singular and impressive solitude: of traffic there is little or none; the fields are almost exclusively pasture-land; the villages are usually distant; of gentlemen's seats there are few, and these are generally afar off; the mills are principally situated on 'back-water'; and but for the cottages, nearly all of which are peasant hostelries, which, in their immediate relation to the locks and weirs, necessarily stand on the river-bank, with now and then a ferry-house, the whole of the landscape for nearly forty miles from the river-source would seem as completely denuded of population as an African desert.

When Harper visited Inglesham fifty years later, he found that the enterprising lock-keeper had jumped onto the tourist band-wagon to supplement his meagre income.

At Inglesham Round House there are plentiful facilities wherewith to refresh the body, and to employ the uncultivated mind; for the lock-keeper's domain includes a number of apologetic sheds and shanties devised for the benefit of picnic-parties; and anything eatable or drinkable likely to be called for by parties on picnic, or boating, or merely padding the hoof, is obtainable, together with the mechanical music of melodeons or other such appliances that will serve you with pennyworths of minstrelsy, or more or less appropriate sauce. Here also is a greatly-patronised camping-ground, generally plentifully occupied with tents in favourable summers.

At about the same time, though, Alfred Williams, who described so vividly the simple life of remote agricultural communities, found that, on

St John's Lock

Lechlade Town

his journey for ROUND ABOUT THE UPPER THAMES, in Lechlade town the rural tradition was continuing very much as it always had.

Today the steeple town is full of bustle and excitement, for it is September Horse Fair. This is usually called 'Flea Fair' or it should be 'Harvest Bug Fair', because about this time harvest bugs disappear from the grass and stubble, and the farm hands and gleaners are no longer tormented with the troublesome insects.

The broad market place in front of the inn and beneath the shade of the spire is packed with horses and people. Farmers and dealers, hands in pockets, stand in groups or saunter round the square, viewing the animals. Here a prospective purchaser opens the mouth of a well-groomed horse to examine its teeth;

another lifts up a fore-foot and scrutinises that, or feels the fetlocks and knees. He is in want of a couple of good horses, for Poppet is getting a little ancient, and Colonel has a nasty limp on the near hind leg, and there is extra work to be done this autumn. But the bidding will be keen, and the farmer is considering whether or not he will be justified in making the outlay, though he knows something must be done.

There are several types of yeomen about the square and some individuals who have come from afar off, for the horse fair is attended by breeders and dealers from many of the Western Counties. There is the tall bronzed son of Somersetshire, with highly distinctive dialect; the bluff and hearty moonraker, dwelling near the breezy downs, spruce and clean shaven, or with stiff, bristling moustache and side-beard; the comfortable-looking Berkshire man; the thin-featured, gentlemanly Oxonian, and the short, sturdy, thick-set man of Gloucestershire, whose home is upon the strong-blowing Cotswolds. In addition to them are the loiterers and sightseers — the wooden-legged pensioner rigged in Sunday best; the town tailor, crippled in both feet; to be sure, the old blacksmith of ninety years, who has absented himself from the forge today in order to note the condition of the horses and the fashion in which they are shod.

Higher up the broad street are vans and vehicles with materials for constructing the merry-go-rounds, coconut shies, and stalls for gingerbreads and knick-knacks. They stand in lines, waiting for the horses to be sold, which will be by noon or soon after. When the dealers have finished they will occupy the square and the space before the inns, and the travellers will exhibit their wares for the young men, women, and children to buy. The afternoon and evening will be devoted to pleasure. Then the people will flock in from the villages round about and the streets will be full to overflowing.

Hart's Weir, Eaton Hastings

From Lechlade it is but a short distance across the flood-plain meadows to the first pound lock on our journey to the sea. It was built in 1790 to bypass the ancient flash lock or navigation weir which stood on the downstream side of the arches of St John's Bridge. A number of pound locks were built on the Upper Thames at this time to improve the navigation for barges using the canal. When William Senior arrived here nearly a century later he found that the lock had so far escaped Conservancy modernization and he was able to view the simple pastoral scene with a contented condescending eye.

The Highworth road is carried by a substantial one-arch bridge over the river at Lechlade, and in the fields, half a mile below,

we arrive at the first lock on the Thames. There are a lock-house and garden to rest in, Thames Conservancy notices to be read, and ancient lock-keeping folk to talk with. It is a very old lock. In the natural order of things it cannot last much longer, and at no distant date, no doubt, it will give place to one of the more useful, but infinitely more prosaic affairs of iron, with modern improvements in the machinery, which the Conservancy supplies when it is necessary to replace the original structures. The partly decayed boards, the hand-rail rising from their outer edge, the lock gates patched many a time, and thinned in regard to their outer casing by many a winter flood, have done their work, and stand in weather-worn picturesqueness, all awry, doing their remaining duty as best they may . . . In the meadow is a big hawthorn on which the hips are already forming, and on a hot summer day the dairy kine will find shelter, lazily flicking the flies from their hides. Haycocks are plentiful on all sides. Yonder the men are hoisting a load of sweet-smelling hay upon the rick. Farther in the distance a late crop is falling in regular swathes; and when the gurgle of water escaping from the dilapidated lock-gates moderates for a moment we can hear the mower whetting his scythe. . . There is something of the semblance of a weir at St John's Bridge, although it is of the most rudimentary kind, having fallen naturally into decay, and even into desuetude. Still, the small sluices are occasionally lifted, and serviceable streams are formed to keep the pool in motion, and prevent the patriarchal trout from giving notice to quit.

Most of the small weirs above Oxford mentioned by early Victorian travellers were still flash weirs, sometimes called flash locks. These were part of a very ancient system by which, during low-water conditions, craft passed through mill-dams and fishing weirs, and over shallow parts of the river with a 'flash' or flush of water sent from the upper reaches.

Radcot Bridge and the Swan Inn

Below Oxford, modern pound locks had replaced nearly all flash locks by the nineteenth century; but in 1862 a total of fifteen still existed on the upper river. Most had old thatched cottages adjoining them which were the homes of the weir keepers, who supplemented their incomes by setting fish traps, wild-fowling, and cutting osiers and rushes. Part of the cottage was often an ale-house. In 1847 James Thorne briefly described them in his Thames volume of RAMBLES BY RIVERS, and then only for the benefit of the artistically minded.

By some of the locks and weirs there are rude thatched cottages with a variety of sheds and lean-tos stuck against them, and a bit of bright flower garden on one side, and oars, eel-pots, and nets are hung about the walls and palings, making the place look as if altogether laid out for the sketcher.

By 1875, when H.R. Robertson came sketching for LIFE ON THE UPPER THAMES, many of the remaining flash weirs and an ancient and unique way of life had been swept away. Under his sketch of a fisherman's fireside, Robertson adds just a glimpse of the hard but independent lives of the people of the Upper Thames.

The interior . . . is one of the few still remaining near the river, with the roomy chimney-corner, massive beams, and stoutly built walls, that really defy the winter's cold, however severe it may be. And it *is* severe in the flat, marshy districts of the Upper Thames; the long continuance of flood, which often imprisons the inmates for months together, renders the comfort of the fireside a consideration of unusual importance. The only one of the household who, during these periods, stirs out at all, is the master himself, with his great boots that reach half way up his thighs. He can thus disregard the foot or two of water that covers the meadows near his home. While he is perhaps looking after the wild-fowl, at this season comparatively abundant, his wife or daughter will be busy making the nets with which, when the waters subside, the fishing will be recommenced.

Although pound locks, with water-level-control weirs alongside them, replaced most of the flash weirs, several continued in use into the twentieth century. Eynsham, Kings and Medley were used until 1927; Hart's Weir at Eaton Hastings was the last to be removed in 1937. C.G. Harper uses Hart's Weir to explain the system which had been used as a matter of course by bargemen for generations but which appeared to be a terrible hazard to some of the pleasure-boating public.

Rushey Weir

Hart's Weir, or Eaton Weir, as the Conservancy elects rather to style it, is but a mile-and-a-quarter below Buscot, and is one of the few old-fashioned weirs, fitted with paddles and rymers, of which a few are removed for the passage of a boat, that now remain. Beside it stands the Anchor inn, with not another house in sight, and the little church of Eaton Hastings – it would be an affectation to speak of the village, unless a few scattered cottages may so be named – two miles away, by the riverside, but so hidden that its existence is not suspected by passing oarsmen.

It is amusing to observe the blank puzzlement that overspreads the faces, and governs the actions, of those occupants of boats from Lechlade who, coming for the first time to this unfamiliar type of weir and lock combined, helplessly steer from one side of the river to the other, in search of the familiar lock-cut and lock-gates, and, failing to find them (as well they may, for such things do not exist here), at last landing and enquiring for them at the inn. Eaton Weir is one of the last now left of the old weirs that served the turn of the river in days of old, and they are, therefore, now so uncommon that none need feel ashamed of coming unexpectedly for the first time to one, and not comprehending the situation. But those who are taken by surprise here and cannot understand why they can find no way through, do, it is evident by leisured observation, feel a kind of shame at being so completely 'sold'. Eaton Weir, and others of its kind, are, in fact, complete barriers across the river, affording a check to all craft until four or five of the paddles are pulled up. The construction is simple, consisting of a sill, generally a heavy beam of wood, laid across the bed of the river, with a similar beam crossing immediately over it, from bank to bank. These form the framework of the weir, which is completed by a number of stout supports (rymer posts) going perpendicularly down at intervals from upper beam to lower, and by a continuous row of 'paddles' set between them. The 'paddles' are, roughly speaking, in the shape of shovels, but much longer in the handle and bigger in the blade. It is obvious that when all the paddles are down in their places the head of water must be considerably raised above the weir, although a volume of water pours through all the whole. To admit the passage of a boat, the weir-keeper draws up four paddles or more, and then, if the craft be going downstream, it is guided by the steersman carefully to the weir, and deftly allowed to be shot through by the force of the waterfall thus created in the opening. A little mild excitement generally accompanies this 'shooting the rapids', even though the fall be only about eighteen inches to two feet when the paddles are first drawn,

Duxford

and reduced to almost nothing if you wait a few minutes while the head of accumulated water runs itself away. The Thames Conservancy will have its dues, and whether it be a lock or a weir you pass, you render threepence for a small boat, and receive a pink ticket in return.

We continue to follow the meandering river, and if our journey is in 1896 or after, we pass through Grafton Lock. Prior to that date we would *have to negotiate a little flash weir called New Weir. A short distance past medieval Radcot Bridge and the Swan Inn is Radcot Lock, also very new, being opened in 1891. Historian Fred Thacker stated that the lock was built on the site of the original flash weir, but in fact that was situated 200 metres or so below, where Old Man's Foot-bridge now spans the stream. The weir had many different names, possibly of past keepers, attached to it, including Clarke's, Bucks and Harper's. There is a delightful engraving of the weir and cottage by Cooke and Owen.*

Newbridge

W.G. Fearnside wrote about Radcot Weir and its function, with a description of the 'picturesque' scene here and further downstream at Rushey Lock, one of the 1790 series of new pound locks.

The weirs are always connected with various accessory circumstances, as the mill, the fisherman's hut, or the cottage of the person who collects the tolls: breaking the line of the river, they heighten and vary the character of the scene, which is increased by the water in parts spouting through the apertures of the flood-gates, in others, fretting among the mossy timbers, or rushing over aquatic plants that cling to the framework; and thus, broken into a thousand rills, continue the current of the river. Clarke's Weir forms a very picturesque example of these necessary appendages to the navigation. On the right, the landscape continues picturesque while, on the other bank, the line of country is flat and uninteresting. The river, after passing a small weir with merely a hut, designated Old Nan's Weir, and forming various curvatures, reaches Rushy Weir and Lock, where the stream, gliding between shady trees, pursues its course to the right; but a cut, or small canal with a lock, has been made to the left for the convenience of barges. The *coup d'oeil* of the islet on which the house of the keeper of the lock is situated, sheltered with foliage, and the water clear and unruffled, adding to the serenity of the scene, creates a charming rustic picture.

Ten years after Fearnside passed by, the lock was 'in a most frightful state of dilapidation. It had only two gates out of four, and it was stuffed up with hurdles, and straw.' It was not completely rebuilt until 1898.

The countryside through which the Thames passes is formed of alluvial deposits laid down by the river and its tributaries over thousands of years. Many areas are low-lying and subject to flooding. At the beginning of the Victorian period the riverside lands were still being farmed in the traditional way; they were mainly pastures used as summer grazing, or rich, peaty meadows, a botanist's paradise, cut for hay. Between Radcot and Newbridge, for instance, thousands of acres were unenclosed and undrained Common Land, often a spongy morass frequented only by the wildfowler. An Enclosure Act for this area was passed in 1848 and a Drainage Act in 1866. Since that time much of it has succumbed to the plough, pesticides, herbicides and fertilizers.

In the 1870s the influential Squire Campbell of Buscot had chivied the Conservancy into making sufficient repairs to this part of the river to enable his barges to take cargoes of distilled beet spirit through to

London. A few narrow boats from the Oxford Canal were also making their way upstream via the Duke's Cut, which connects the canal with the Thames near King's Lock, to unload coal at Newbridge Wharf.

At Ridge's Weir, also called Hart's, a mile below Newbridge, Mrs Ridge, the keeper, was allowed one shilling for passing through each canal boat, and four pence for any pleasure boat. The trade certainly did not earn her a living. The weir was removed and replaced by a foot-bridge in 1879, but the ancient thatched house, part of St John's College estates, continued to be occupied into the 1950s. Parts of side sluices and house foundations can still be seen among the tangled thicket of willow, blackthorn and forlorn fruit trees.

Two miles below once stood Ark Weir, similar to Ridge's, but mouldering away sometime before the other's demise. These two flash weirs were eventually replaced on a new site halfway between them by Northmoor Lock which was opened in 1898. The next feature in the otherwise fairly featureless riverscape, is the ancient site of Bablock Hythe – 'hythe' meaning wharf. But Bablock is more noted for its ferry, first recorded in the fifteenth century and, before the days of the motor vehicle, an important crossing for local farmers and traders. William Senior takes up the description, but do not expect to find his inn there now. From here he takes us on to Godstow, and to within sight of Oxford.

Bablock Hythe Ferry

Although Bablock Hythe by road is no more than five miles from Oxford, the circuitous voyage by the River Thames is twelve miles. Bablock Hythe is a well-known station on the Upper Thames, although it does not boast the rank of hamlet or village, and has for the accommodation of man and beast only one of the small old-fashioned inns of the humblest sort, where the rooms are low, the beams big and solid, the floors flagged, and the apartments fitted up with all manner of three-corner cupboards and antique settles. The great ferry-boat, however, gives it a decided position of importance, and it is known to Thames tourists principally as the starting point for visiting either Cumnor or Stanton Harcourt. . . . The Thames takes a northerly course from Bablock Hythe, and winds and doubles in such contortions that in one part a strip of not more than twelve yards of meadow separates two reaches of considerable length. A high, wide wooden bridge, bearing the name of Skinner's Weir, now crosses our course, and soon we come to Pinkhill Lock, so called from a farm of that name in the

Skinners Weir

Godstow Bridge

neighbourhood. The weir is a new one and a great contrast in its severe and formal cut to the weather-worn structures to which we have been accustomed. The lock-house is quite a dainty cottage, and the garden one of the prettiest to be found along the Thames. The lock garden is generally a winsome little preserve, with its kitchen garden, flower beds, sometimes a beehive, its stack of fagots, and a general air of rusticity; the lock-keeper, or probably his wife, at Pinkhill Weir has devoted special care and attention to a flower bed running the whole length of the lock, which I found to be bordered by a blaze of summer flowers. From the lock bridge a commanding view is obtained of the hilly country to the right, and the woods and copses around its base, and straggling to the top.

Three miles from Eynsham we are at Godstow Bridge. The spire of Cassington Church, a conspicuous landmark on the left hand throughout, is a pleasanter object by far than the tall chimneys on the right, which are not redeemed by the rows of poplars that would fain hide them. It is unfortunate, but true, that the first glimpses we get of the spires of Oxford are in conjunction with the tall red-brick chimney and not elegant University paper mills. While following the bend at the broad part of the river the public buildings of beautiful Oxford open one by one into view, but again disappear temporarily at the next bend, at the head of which stands King's Weir. This serves as much the purposes of a lock as a weir, its gates opening when necessary to admit the passage of larger craft than those which can be conveyed over the roller supplied for pleasure-boats. The river from the pool is almost choked with weeds, very narrow, and of hardly sufficient depth at low water to admit the passage of an ordinary pleasure-boat . . . The farther arch of the old bridge at Godstow has been removed to admit various improvements being carried out on the branch of the stream, which here divides, and in order to widen the structure; but the two arches of the ascent from the right-hand side remain as they were, and the well-known Trout Inn at Godstow retains all its characteristics of creepers, flowers, tiled roof, and pleasant waterside seats. A full view of Oxford, set back beyond the farthest confines of Port Meadow is obtained, while the smell of the roses in the pretty garden still lingers about us. The village of Wolvercott lies to the left, and at the end of the mill-stream, the entrance of which was noticed just above King's Weir. Close by the ivy-covered gable of the nunnery, a new weir is being erected; and it may be added that in the excavations incidental to the work four old stone coffins were discovered in the summer of 1885.

Pinkhill Lock

King's Weir

The reach between Godstow and Medley, skirting the vast area of Common Land known as Port Meadow, has long been the aquatic playground for the townspeople and University of Oxford. It became especially popular in the Victorian Age after the Bossoms and the Beesleys – families that had been associated with the river for centuries – established boat stations at Medley Weir, just outside the town, where they carried out the building and hiring out of punts, skiffs and sailing boats by the dozen. A third man, Theo Smith, specialized in building sailing canoes and boats. Few commercial craft then used this shallow reach but bypassed it through the Oxford Canal and its connecting cuts. Small pleasure-craft moving up from the town could be dragged over the rollers alongside Medley Weir if it was closed.

Former undergraduates have written nostalgically of the occasions spent skating on the frozen meadow and sailing or rowing to the Perch, or Trout Inn, perhaps for spiced beer and a game of skittles. Sadly much of the beautiful scenery they described has been spoilt by the demands of human leisure activities; the once-luxuriant beds of reeds, rushes and other water plants have been swept away by the wash thrown up by motor launches, such as the high-speed coaching craft following rowing crews on this popular practice course. The reach is one of the few on the upper river where dinghy sailing is possible, but to a lesser degree than in Victorian times because of the City Council's planting of rows of alien hybrid poplar trees which make an effective wind break.

Medley Weir

Medley boat station

CHAPTER TWO

Oxford to Reading

In Victorian times the river's approach to Oxford, past Osney, and the site of its once magnificent abbey, had already been spoilt by railways, terraced housing, factories, mills and gasworks. But once through Folly Bridge, or Grand Pont, the scene, although artificial, improves to a broad straight reach leading towards Iffley, bordered by Christ Church Meadow. Here the river's volume is increased by a third from the waters of the River Cherwell. At Folly Bridge there were once wharves for barges carrying essential supplies to and from London. Here too the Thames began for many Victorians – for sport, exploration, leisure and social occasion.

When Mr and Mrs Hall arrived here in the 1850s, they first had to pass by a weir and through a lock which had been built in one of the bridge arches. It was removed in 1884 but its walls may still be seen in the arch behind Salter's landing stage. The Halls describe the early days of the Upper Thames passenger boat industry, although, with mere horse-power, excursions only proceeded as far as Nuneham. A few of those early 'houseboats', some of them redundant ceremonial barges of the City of London Livery Companies, lived on into the 1960s as static features moored on Christ Church Meadow. Here they were used by individual colleges during rowing occasions but they have since been replaced by a dismal row of college boat-houses.

We are below Folly Bridge, having passed through the lock, which terminates the right branch of the river: there is a fall here of about three feet. A tavern, situated on a sort of quay, and a block of warehouses, sufficiently mark the locality, but the latter unfortunately interrupts the passage onto the street from the beautiful grounds of Christ Church. Christ Church Meadow, with its embowered 'walks', has been famous for ages; it is the public promenade; and necessarily here, or at the quay alluded to, boats are always numerous, for this is almost the only place in the vicinity in which there are conveniences for boating.

As will be supposed, the boats are of all sorts and sizes, from the huge and elaborately decorated pleasure-barge, to the thin, light rowing boat, that looks like a line upon the water. We must pause awhile to give some description of these conveyances upon the great highway of the Thames, for, from Oxford, the river is of value for passage and traffic.

For smaller parties, of about twenty or thirty, Oxford is abundantly supplied with boats which are known by the name of 'houseboats'. The interior is a spacious room; while 'the deck' affords opprtunities for viewing the scenery and enjoying the pleasant breezes of the river – being served with benches for the convenience of such as prefer the open air, and having a light iron balustrade around. These boats are leisurely towed up and down the river by horses, and are, in fact, large and broad barges, within which the 'house' is constructed, with its windows and gaily painted or gilded panels. Seats surround the interior, and a table, generally bountifully spread, occupies the

Osney Lock, Oxford

centre. Recently some have been built – and are in use – to accommodate large parties, not infrequently as many as two hundred persons, who often dance quadrilles on the deck.

Two decades on G. Davis at St Helen's Works, Abingdon, built the screw-driven saloon passenger steamer Thames, *and possibly its sister ship, the* Isis. *A company with offices at Abingdon, possibly Davis's own company, began a regular weekly service from Kingston to Oxford and back. Passengers paid 18s. (90p) single, or £1. 10s. (£1.50) return for the complete distance, staying overnight at Windsor and Reading. They could also join at intermediate towns, where the steamer would wait for passengers arriving by train. Within a few years, Salter Bros., originally based at University Boat-house, had acquired premises at Folly Bridge and incorporated the Kingston steamer run into their boat-building and hire business. They eventually acquired or built a large fleet of steamers, maintaining the regular Kingston run up to the*

Beesley's osier yard, Upper Fisher Row, Oxford

The view from Folly Bridge

Oxford College barges

late 1960s. Other companies along the river had been building and running excursion steam boats too. At Folly Bridge, James Porter also capitalized on the new craze for steam by employing several small paddle-driven boats for trips which probably went no further than Nuneham and back.

While some went for mechanical forms of locomotion, others opted for more strenuous and individualistic outdoor activities. The world depicted in Jerome's THREE MEN IN A BOAT had begun and countless rowing parties embarked at Folly Bridge and headed downstream. The ladies were by no means out-done; Elizabeth Robins Pennell, with husband, Joseph, on their STREAM OF PLEASURE journey in 1891, seems to have naively but bravely faced the elements, perhaps with more equanimity than Jerome's crew.

It was pouring in torrents, on the morning of the 1st of August, when we drove from 'The Mitre' down to Salter's boat-house at the appointed hour. Our boat, which was brand new and had not yet been launched, was not ready, and Salter's men seemed surprised to see us. This showed that the weather was even worse than we thought it, and the outlook more hopeless. And yet, during the couple of hours we waited on the rain-soaked raft, two or three other pleasure parties started out in open boats. The girls in the stern, wrapped in mackintoshes and huddled under umbrellas, and the men at the sculls, their soaked flannels clinging to them, looked so miserably wet that we felt for the first time how very superior our boat was.

It was only a pair-oared skiff, shorted and broader than those generally seen on the Thames – 'a family boat,' an old river man called it with contempt; but then it had a green waterproof canvas cover which stretched over three iron hoops and converted it for all practical purposes into a small, a very small, house-boat. By a complicated arrangement of strings the canvas could be so rolled up and fastened on top as – theoretically – not to interfere with our view of the river banks on bright days; or it could be let down to cover the entire boat from stern to bow – an umbrella by day, a hotel by night.

Under it we could camp out without the bother of pitching a tent. We had already talked a great deal about the beautiful nights upon the river, when we should go to bed with the swans and rise up with the larks, and cook our breakfast under the willows, and wash our dishes and ourselves in quiet clear pools. What if river inns were as extortionate and crowded as they are said to be? we should have our own hotel with us wherever we went. In the midst of a weak and damp hurrah from one ancient boatman, and under a heavy baptism not of champagne, but of rain, the *Rover* was at last pushed off her trestles and with one vigorous shove sent clean across the

Oriel College barge during May Eights Week

Iffley Lock and Mill

Sandford Lock and Paper Mill

Thames to the raft where we stood under umbrellas, while Salter's men at once began to load her with kitchen and bedroom furniture. They provided us with an ingenious stove with kettles and frying-pans fitting into each other like the pieces of a Chinese puzzle, a lantern, cups and saucers and plates, knives and forks and spoons, a can of alcohol, and, for crowning comfort, a mattress large enough for a double bedstead. It filled the boat from stern to bow, covering the seats,

burying the sculls and boat hooks, bulging out through and over the rowlocks. It was clear if it went we must stay, and so we said, as if we rather liked the prospect of roughing it, that we could manage just as well and be just as comfortable if we slept on our rugs; for we carried all the Roman blankets and steamer rugs we possessed, together with a lot of less decorative blankets borrowed from our landlady in London, and the bundle they made took up the place of two people in the boat. The locker

The flood relief weir at Sandford. A few identical Victorian structures are still in use

Nuneham

was stored with our supply of sardines, jam, chocolate, tea, sugar, biscuits, towels, and tea-cloths. Our bags were stowed away with the kitchen things. And then at last we crawled into the long green tunnel.

For much of the nineteenth century, day trippers from Oxford had headed down through Iffley and Sandford locks, to reach one of the most delightful picnic spots on the whole river, situated by ancient thatched cottages that nestled under the woods and parkland at Nuneham. The cottages and the bridge to the island at Nuneham marked the site of a flash lock which fell out of use at the beginning of the century. The park had been laid out by Capability Brown, therefore many writers extolled the beauty of the situation, sometimes to excess. We, however, shall have the slightly acid pen of Charles Harper in 1910, rather than one of the 'picturesque English landscape' word pictures loved by the Victorians.

Everyone knows Nuneham, for does not Salter, who runs his comfortable steamboats between Oxford and Richmond, drop passengers here, on the banks, and does he not call and pick them up again at the close of the day, conveying them from Oxford and back at the cost of one shilling? Yea; thousands have made that trip; and, given a fine day, there is, *experto crede*, not any trip more delightful. But if the day turn tearful, then Nuneham is the very last place to which any one who is not a fish or a duck would wish to go. Do I not know the misery of it at such times: the landing on the wet, clayey bank under the trees of the glorious woods, which shed great spattering drops of rain on one; the half-mile walk, or rather, butter-slide, by the woodland track, to the picturesque thatched cottage in the lovely backwater, where the cottagers in fine weather supply open-air teas to these pilgrims, and in wet weather do the like, refusing, much to the said pilgrims' disgust, to give them the much-needed shelter in their own dry and comfortable quarters; with the result that those unhappy persons grow cold and shivery and develop colds in their heads, and entertain savage thoughts of Nuneham? Truly, no more miserable experience is possible than that of sitting in one of the picturesquely thatched arbours by the waterside, and dallying over a lukewarm tea, awaiting the hour for the up-river steamer's arrival, while the moisture-laden wind comes searchingly in at the open front. And it does not make matters better to know that those disobliging cottagers are, all the while, crouching over their own roaring wood-log fires.

But let us dwell no longer upon these harrowing experiences. It does not always rain at Nuneham – but only when we want to go there. Then it rains all day. But when the sun shines, Nuneham is the ideal place for an idle day, and those draughty arbours the most exquisite of nooks. From them you look out upon a river scene that closely resembles some stage 'set'. The

St Helen's Wharf, Abingdon

trees, right and left, or, to speak in stage conventional language – on-prompt and off-prompt sides – hang in that almost impossibly picturesque way we expect in the first act of a melodrama of the old Adelphi or Drury Lane type. You know the kind of thing; or, if you do not, go to Nuneham and see it. Anyway, take my word for it, that this is sheerly competitive with the stage. Beneath these trees, whose other side, you are quite convinced, is merely canvas and framework, are the usual conventional rocks, on one of which the villain will presently sit

Skating on the Thames at Abingdon

and gloat over the impending fall of the hero. And swans come lazily paddling up to the rush-fringed margin of the river; and, really, all you miss is the limelight.

We slip back in time again for a quarter of a century, to where J. Penderel-Brodhurst in THE ROYAL RIVER picks up the tiller lines and steers us onward to Abingdon, through its lock and bridge, with St Helen's elegant spire framed in its arches.

The Berkshire shore is lined with pleasant houses for half a mile or so below Abingdon Bridge. The towing-path is here upon the Oxford bank, and skirts rich meadows picturesquely studded with large shade-trees. Away to the left lie heavy masses of woodland, such as engirdle the whole of the Thames Valley; on the facing bank are the straggling environs of Abingdon, having, when seen from this point, somewhat of the foreign aspect so often worn by these little waterside towns. But in less than a mile we are amid scenes that are very English. The meadows at first are flat, which, rather than a blemish, I esteem to be a beauty. The perfection of sylvan and pastoral river scenery, as distinguished from the bold and rocky loveliness of some of our wilder English streams, demands flattish banks, the better to throw into relief the undulating fields and shimmering woodlands which so often close in a homely scene having for relief merely some grey church tower almost hidden among the lofty elms, and the mellowed ruddiness of a farmhouse gable. A little below Abingdon the tiny Ock enters the stream, and so ends its independent existence. Any time from eight to ten in the morning – for, oddly enough, boating-men are rarely up with the lark – camping-out parties may be seen engaged in the serious business of breakfasting, or in the lighter but less exhilarating task of washing-up the cups and saucers, and generally 'making tidy' before the day's leisurely pull. As a rule,

Culham Lock

however, the river is deserted during the whole of the forenoon, even in the height of the season, as, indeed, the towing-path always is, whether it be late or early – at least, upon this portion of the stream. The river banks, from the bridge at Abingdon to Culham Lock, are very charming in summer, to those who are content with ordinary scenery, and do not expect a famous view on entering every reach. Nearing Culham, the river bends very sharply to the right, and just at the curve a white wooden bridge crosses a beautiful little back-water, brilliantly pied with water-lilies, and thickly bordered with graceful aquatic grasses. Then come fields of standing corn, the sturdy ears sheltering the frail crimson poppies – wheat and tares intermingled. From some hidden spot in the

The Old Weir at Day's Lock

centre of the field comes the loud, harsh cry of the corncrake, that bird so often heard and so seldom seen. Sometimes the crop is the drooping oats or the 'bold and bearded barley'; but whatever be the grain, there is the fat, solemn rook, who reluctantly wheels away from his farinaceous banquet, to hide for a few minutes in the long row of elms in the adjoining field. Close to Culham the stream divides, a broad rushy channel flowing past Sutton Courtney, with its venerable Edwardian Manor House and the well-known weirs, while a straight, narrow, and not very picturesque cut, makes direct for the Lock. . . .

Between Clifton and Day's Lock the country is remarkably solitary. The waterside meadows are nearly all empty; but here and there a herd of cattle browses leisurely, or, if it be high noon, shelters itself from the heat and the tormenting flies under the lee of the thick hedgerows. Pedestrians are never seen. That it is good to row upon a beautiful river, but undesirable to walk by the side of it, appears to be the popular idea; but despite the physical exhilaration and the aesthetic delight of the rhythmical swing of oars, the river can be seen best from the towing-path, and if the love of walking-tours had not very largely died out we might expect to see the banks of the Upper Thames as much frequented as its waters. It is often possible to pass between Clifton and Day's Lock without meeting either man or boat, which seems a little odd, since that reach is in high favour during the season. To the walker upon the towing-path this silence and vacancy become oppressive, and the sudden splash of a water-rat striking out from among the rushes is quite startling. The Berkshire shore is flattish here; but there are swelling uplands beyond, and the Wrekin-shaped Sinodun Hill looms quite close upon the left. Presently there stands out from among the trees on the Oxford bank an old church with a very long nave and tall tower, with an unusual high-pitched red roof, topped by a vane. That is the famous Abbey Church of Dorchester, the solitary remnant of the ancient grandeur of the olden capital of Wessex. A little farther is Day's Lock, with the ferry between Little Wittenham and Dorchester, where, even in a season of drought, the water is unusually full and brimming, the result, perhaps, of the wedding nearby of the little Thame with the more classic and magnificent Thames, or Isis, as the poets have preferred to call it. This conceit owes its origin almost entirely to such comparatively modern poets as Warton and Drayton, though Spenser, in the *FAERIE QUEENE*, seems to have originated the legend in somewhat of a back-handed way:

Day's Lock and Wittenham Clumps

The lovely bridegroom came,
The noble Thamis, with all his goodly traine,
But before him there went, as best became,
His auncient parents, namely, th' auncient Thame;
But much more aged was his wife than he,
The Ouze, whom men doe Isis rightly name.
Full weak and crooked creature seemed shee,
And almost blind through Eld, that scarce her way could see.

Spenser certainly had his geography wrong if he thought that the Bedfordshire River Ouse formed the upper part of the Thames. The fact remains that nowhere in early records does the name Isis occur as an alternative to Thames. Saxon land charters and later official documents mentioning the river from Thames Head downwards, always call it the Thames, although spellings vary.

Passing under the towing-path bridge across the mouth of the Thame we row up the pretty winding stream to the ancient town of Dorchester.

Here, penning back the current, stand the great Abbey Mills, where C.J. Cornish, in THE NATURALIST ON THE THAMES, educates us on the mysteries of milling and commercial fish-taking – a part of the real world of the working Thames unknown to most of the passing pleasure-seekers.

Fish and flour go together as bye-products of nearly all our large rivers. The combination comes about thus: wherever there is a water-mill, a mill cut is made to take the water to it. The larger the river, the bigger and deeper the mill cut and dam, unless the mill is built across an arm of the stream itself. This mill-dam, as every trout-fisher knows, holds the biggest fish, and where there are no trout, or few trout, it will be full of big fish, while in the pool below there are perhaps as many more. Of all the food fishes of our rivers the eel is really by far the most important. He flourishes everywhere, in the smallest pools and brooks as well as in the largest rivers, and grows up to a weight of 9 lb or 10 lb, and sometimes, though rarely, more. His price indicates his worth, and never falls below 10*d*. per pound. Consequently he is valuable as well as plentiful and the millers know this well. On nearly all rivers the millers have eel-traps, some of the ancient sort being 'bucks', made of withes, and worked by expensive, old-fashioned machinery like the mill gear. Another and most paying dodge of the machine-made order is worked in the mill itself, and makes an annexe to the mill-wheel.

I once spent an agreeable hour watching the making of barley meal and the catching of eels, literally side by side. It was sufficiently good fun to make me put my gun away for the afternoon, and give up a couple of hours' walk with the chance of a duck, to watch the mill and eel-traps working.

They were both in a perfect old-world bye-end of the Thames Valley, in the meads at the back of the forgotten but perfect abbey of the third order at Dorchester, under the tall east

window of which the River Thame was running bank full, fringed with giant poplars, from which the rooks were flying to look at their last year's nests in the abbey trees.

The mill was, as might be supposed, the Abbey Mill; but on driving up the lane I was surprised to see how good and large was the miller's house, a fine dwelling of red and grey brick; and what a length of frontage the old mill showed, built of wood, as most of them are, but with two sets of stones, and space for two wheels. Only one was at work, and that was grinding barley-meal – meal from nasty, foreign barley full of dirt; but the miller had English barley-meal too, soft as velvet and sweet as a new-baked loaf. Stalactites of finest meal dust hung from every nail, peg, cobweb, and rope end on the walls, fine meal strewed the floor, coarse meal poured from the polished shoots, to which the sacks hung by bright steel hooks, and on both floors ancient grindstones stood like monuments of past work and energy, while below and beside all this dust and floury dryness roared the flooded waters of the dam and the beating floats of the wheel. 'Have you any eels?' I asked. 'Come and see,' said the miller.

He stopped his wheel, unbolted the door, and we looked up the mill dam, two hundred yards long, straight as a line, embanked by double rows of ancient yews, the banks made and the trees planted by the monks five hundred years ago. Then we stepped into the wheel-house, where the water, all yellow and foaming, was pouring into two compartments set with iron gratings below, on which it rose and foamed. Seizing a long pole with prongs like walrus teeth, the miller felt below the water on the bars. 'Here's one, anyway,' he said, and by a dexterous haul scooped up a monster eel onto the floor. In a box which he hauled from the dam he had more, some of 5 lb weight, which had come down with the flood – an easy and profitable fishery, for the eels can lie in the trap till he hauls

Overy, or Dorchester Abbey Mill

them out, and sell well summer and winter. It pays as well as a poultry yard. Once he took a 9 lb fish; 2½ lb to 4 lb are common.

Another dodge for taking eels, which is not in the nature of what is called a 'fixed engine', is the movable eel-trap or 'grig wheel'. It is like a crayfish basket and is, in fact, the same thing, only rather larger. They can be obtained from that old river hand, Mr Bambridge, at Eton, weighted, stoppered, and ready for use, for 7s. 6d. each, and unweighted for 5s. They are neat wickerwork tunnels, with the usual contrivance at the mouth to make the entrance of the eels agreeable and their exit impossible. The 'sporting' side of these traps is that a good deal of judgement is needed to set them in the right places in a river. Many people think that eels like carrion and favour mud. Mr Bambridge says his experience is different and his 'advice to those about to fish' with this kind of eel-trap is suggestive of new ideas about eels. He says that 'for bait nothing can beat about a dozen and a half of small or medium live gudgeon, failing these large minnows, small dace, roach, loach, etc., though in some streams about a dozen good bright large lob worms, threaded on a copper wire and suspended inside, are very effective, and should always be given a trial. Offal I have tried but found useless, eels being a cleaner feeding fish than many are aware of; and feeding principally in gravelly, weedy parts, the basket should be well tucked up under a long flowing weed, as it is to these places they go for food, such as the ground fish, loach, miller's thumb, crayfish, shrimps, mussels, etc. . . .'

Meanwhile, the Pennells, after setting off from Oxford in rain, probably had a fast and adventurous passage on a swollen river, nearly coming to grief under Abingdon Bridge in the swift current. Perhaps that is why, before moving on to Wallingford, they decided to spend a

Clifton Hampden

whole weekend at the little village of Clifton Hampden, where the riverside appears to have been as busy with holiday-makers as any seaside town.

We got to Clifton Hampden on Friday evening; all day long on Saturday there was a constant going and coming. We never went out on the road between the inn and the river that we did not meet a stream of men in flannels and bright blazers; women in blue serges, gay blouses and sailor hats, on their way to the 'Barley Mow'. We never went to the landing-place that we did not see launches and skiffs and punts (and once the *Minnehaha* and the *Hiawatha*, two real canoes) either passing by or pulling to the shore where the pretty girl was ready with her boat-hook. It was strange how even the record-breakers, at other landing-places in such a hurry to be off, found time to stop and

The Barley Mow Inn

help her, or to watch her as she skilfully punted her way in and out of the great mass of boats, put some under the bridge for the night, brought out others for the crews about to start.

Here all was life and movement, while Clifton Hampden itself, where the thatched cottages are scattered along the elm-shaded road, and climb to the church high above the river, seemed to sleep peacefully day and night. Only the schoolhouse, with its large clock-face and loud bell, gave signs of life. If you went into the Post Office, where sour balls and ink-bottles were the chief stock-in-trade, you started a little bell jingling as you opened the door; but it was five minutes or more before the postmaster came in from the near fields, bringing the smell of hay with him. Fishermen slumbered on the river banks, and there was always one punt, stationed almost under the shadow of the little church, in which on three chairs sat three solemn men who never stirred, except when one, still holding fast to his line with his left hand, with his right lifted up a great brown jug, drank long and deep, and handed it to the next, and so it passed to the third. The sun shone, the rain fell, the shadows grew longer and longer and the jug lighter and lighter, but whenever I passed, there they still sat.

By evening so many people had come to the 'Barley Mow' that a dozen or more had to be quartered in the village. The publisher and parson were put in a delightful little cottage, with roses clustering at its door. But we having come first, were given the best chamber – the Honeymoon Room, the landlady called it; and all the afternoon she had kept showing it to the boating parties who had lunched or taken tea with her. 'The lady won't mind', I would hear her say as she opened the door. But evidently the visitors did, for if I looked up it was only to see tall figures in white flannel beating a hasty retreat among the poppies. . . .

We left the 'Barley Mow' on Monday morning under a grey, threatening sky. But it was Bank Holiday, and not even the

Benson Lock

occasional showers could keep the boats at home. Many went by decked with water lilies; tents on shore were gay with flags. Those river fiends, the steam launches, were out in full force, puffing past and tossing us on their waves, and washing the banks on either side. We began to think that after all it is rather aggravating to see the angler aroused from contemplation, the camper interrupted in his dish-washing, the idler disturbed in his drifting, and sometimes the artist and his easel upset, all for people who turn their backs on the beauty of the river and play 'nap' and drink beer or champagne, as they might in the nearest public house or club at home.

The great business of the day with everybody, however, was eating and drinking. The thin blue smoke of camp fires rose above the reeds. In small boats kettles sang and hampers were unpacked. In the launches the cloth was never removed. And in these narrow upper reaches, we could look across the river into camps and boats and see what every man was eating for his dinner.

After Shillingford, where the arches of the bridge framed in the river beyond, and its low island, and the far blue hills, and where, near 'The Swan', 'arry and 'arriet were romping, Benson, a few red roofs straggling landward from a grey pinnacled church tower, came in sight, and to Benson we walked for lunch. The village is at its best seen from a distance; its church is restored into stupidity; its inns, survivals of coaching days, are less picturesque than their associations.

Our resting-place for the night was Wallingford, a town with much history and little to show for it. When we pulled ashore it was raining hard, and we went at once to the old gabled 'George', where we found a German street band and a great crowd, and horses trotting through the courtyard, and occasionally trying to make their way into the Coffee Room. It was the day of the Galloway Races, whatever they may be, and local excitement ran high. The band kept on playing while we ate our tea in company with a party of flannelled record-breakers who were in fine spirits. They blew their own trumpets almost as loud as the cornets outside because they had sculled twenty miles since morning. 'Not bad for a first day out, by Jove, you know!'

The river runs due south from Wallingford for a long six miles (9.5 km) to Goring and Streatley, to where the high, rounded contours of the Berkshire Downs and Chiltern Hills seem to block the river's course, before it slides through the narrow Goring Gap. There is no road bridge in this district, but where the towing-path changes from one side of the river to the other, at Little Stoke and South Stoke, ancient ferries once

Wallingford

existed to transfer bargemen and horses across the river; doubtless also being used as necessary crossings by local villagers and farmers.

The lower of the two ferries connected South Stoke to Moulsford, where the Beetle and Wedge inn is situated, which once provided rest and sustenance for bargemen and towing horses alike, and where, up to the beginning of the twentieth century, wagons occasionally brought timber or grain to the wharf for transfer to barges, which were sometimes still towed by horses. A short distance upstream stands a brash symbol of the age of steam transportation which supplanted much of the commercial river traffic: Brunel's Great Western railway bridge. Here we meet again writer Penderel Brodhurst, to take us via Moulsford to the Victorian playground of the Middle Thames Valley, so convenient to London once the railway had arrived.

Little Stoke Ferry

It is but a short distance hence to the ferry, where the water is remarkably deep and limpid. Opposite thereto is the oddly named 'Beetle and Wedge' Inn, a quaint, three-gabled old place, overgrown with ivy and shaded by clumps of luxuriant elms. 'The Beetle' is a grateful halting-place, and its brick-floored parlour a cool retreat from the glare of the outer world. There is usually a garrulous villager or two, in the long-descended smock-frock beloved of the older generation of peasants even in these changeful days, who will pause in the discussion of their mugs of brown home-brewed to greet the stranger with the old-fashioned courtesy which still happily clings to their class. 'The Beetle and Wedge' is an odd old place, and although not nearly so original as the 'Barley Mow' at Clifton, it has the low

roofs and capacious fireplaces which add so much to the comfort of an ancient hostel. It is really astonishing how large a number of our old wayside inns have survived the crushing blow dealt them by the abolition of the stage-coach. There they stand still, with their venerable gables, handsome red roofs, and ample chimneys, eloquently suggestive of warmth and good cheer for tired travellers. In a comfortable old-fashioned inn the crusty loaf, the hunch of well-seasoned Cheshire, and the tankard with 'a good head to it', like David Copperfield's birthday treat, have a zest and flavour which are always lacking elsewhere; the result, no doubt, of their being usually eaten during the exhilaration following upon physical exercise. These ancient Thames-side inns possess a charm peculiar to themselves, due largely to their lovely surroundings and to the river flowing beneath their windows. . . .

As we near Cleeve Lock the scenery becomes yet more sylvan. The river is densely lined with trees, the more especially on the Oxford shore, and the stream winds just enough for picturesqueness. Groups of splendid beeches dot the country, and the water is enlivened by many a boatful of flannelled rowers and pink-vested sirens. Ladies appear to have recognised, with intuitive taste, that pink and white are two of the most effective colours for river wear, and the Thames, in all the fashionable reaches, owed much of its vivacity to the brilliant hues of its attendant water-nymphs. However solitary the river may be in some parts, as between Clifton and Dorchester, for instance, there is enough of life and movement within hail of Goring. The neighbourhood of Cleeve Lock is a favourite haunt for houseboats and campers, since there is nothing prettier on that side of Abingdon until such famous spots as Henley and Maidenhead are reached. The houseboats which take up their moorings hereabouts are usually of the larger and more elaborate pattern. The little muslined windows are gaily

The Beetle and Wedge Inn, Moulsford

Cleeve Lock

Floods and ice at Goring Lock

decked with flowers, there is a miniature flower-garden upon the flat roof, and where the roof overhangs are suspended Chinese lanterns, gorgeous with many a brilliant stripe and spot. A graceful white-robed figure, in a coquettish pink sash, seated in the stern, is not the least attractive object in the landscape. The roar of the Streatley weirs below is plainly heard, and many are the lovely glimpses of the brimming, rushy river between the lock and the bridge.

Half a mile or so below Cleeve Lock the stream divides, the cut to the left going to Goring Lock and the main channel to Streatley. From the point of divergence to Streatley and Goring Bridge is but a brief pull, and few pilgrims of the Thames will desire to push on without halting for a while at this pretty village. Near the bridge is a mill, fed from the river, looking very picturesque with its steep gables and high-set dormer windows. The weirs here are favourite sketching grounds, and almost daily in summer and early autumn easels are pitched. These weirs are exemplars of the picturesque. Roughly built up with stone and stakes, they are overgrown with furzy vegetation, to which the water, as it pours foaming down the cascade, forms a charming contrast. There are few prettier glimpses of Thames scenery than are to be had from the long white toll-bridge which connects Goring with Streatley. Looking down are the thick woodlands about Cleeve Lock, with the rich, timbered meadows on the Berkshire bank. Upward, towards Goring and Pangbourne, the course of the river is seemingly stemmed by the downs, which are covered with herbage and timbered to the water's edge. The weirs, with their tumbling waters, and the little eyots, cumbered with tall osiers, add to the picturesque diversity of the scene. The twin villages themselves are embosomed in foliage, which in the wane of summer takes many changing tints. Streatley is a delightful place to halt for the night on a boating or walking excursion. Its material advantages are that it has capital accommodation for the tired walker and rower, and that the proximity of Goring Station makes it easy to bring up the heavy luggage, without which ladies are not happy, even on the river. Of its more aesthetic attractions I have already spoken. To the dweller in towns it is unspeakably delicious to be lulled to sleep and gently awakened by the musical plash of the weirs, while a stroll at dusk along the river bank is full of delights. In the gloaming the ruminating, sweet-breathed kine loom mistily as they lie sociably grouped under the lee of a protecting hedge. On the river twinkle through the gathering night the lamps of the houseboats, the Chinese lanterns, depending from the overhanging roofs, glowing through their fantastic filaments like great transparent fire-flies. And but for the rush of the weirs, the dip of a belated oar, and an occasional ring of laughter from the huge, blackly outlined boats, the night is silent.

Streatley Bridge and Church

In the 1880s, the artist George Leslie extolled the beauties of the neighbourhood. He was, however, somewhat vexed by the influx of amateur artists who wished to enjoy the same views as he did.

One cannot wonder at the number of artists who are attracted by the many beauties of Streatley and Goring; the river, the two mills, the bridge, the hill, the eyots and backwaters all lend themselves to the painter's skill, the whole place abounding in rich material for his art. But my pleasure in it, I am ashamed to confess, is considerably lessened by the numbers of sketching tents and white umbrellas that meet the eye, perched on every coign of vantage around this spot: in the sketching season the little coffee room at the Swan has easels and artists' traps in every corner, and the village swarms with geniuses and their wives.

The Swan Hotel, Streatley

Camping out

John Leyland takes us further along the Thames, in THE THAMES ILLUSTRATED (1891), past Hart's Wood, and the islands where a flash lock once barred the stream, to Whitchurch and Pangbourne, reminding us that, in some districts, the Thames still provided a valuable crop of osiers for the basketmaking industry.

The charms of this delightful neighbourhood are by no means confined to the river. The countryside inland is very beautiful, and the road from Reading to Oxford, which is the neighbour of the Thames on the Berkshire side, is remarkably beautiful as it passes over the hill by Basildon to Streatley, affording a glorious view of the winding river beneath the deep slope of Hart's Wood on the other side. There is, too, a romantically beautiful footpath from Whitchurch to Goring on the Oxfordshire bank. It passes along the top of the woods, with a Lover's Leap by the way, and varied and attractive views. The cultivation of osiers for commerce may be noted as a curious and profitable industry along this part of the river, and the osier farms are very pleasant to visit. Not long ago, there was an ancient dame at one of them, whose years were near five-score, but who could strip the rods and bind them as featly as any young one in the crowd. The rods are gathered from the eyots in punts, and are tied up and placed with their roots downward in a protected piece of water, where they shoot afresh, and then, in due season, rapid fingers strip them of their bark by an ingenious method, and they come out the long white rods that are the wickers of commerce, of market baskets and garden chairs, which may all remind us of the Upper Thames.

If Streatley was the Mecca for artists, then Pangbourne and its neighbour, Whitchurch, drew the London anglers. They came in hundreds, tramping from the station, bowed down by great wicker baskets and rod cases, to line Pangbourne Reach for weekend matches,

The Thames from Hart's Wood

or, in twos and threes, to hire punts to fish the eddies between the foaming weirs or mill races and the white painted wooden toll-bridge. The wealthier might book a professional fisherman, complete with bait, tackle and boat; perhaps Ashley from The Swan, where the family not only provided all facilities for fishermen and boating parties, but also owned several barges which brought coal to Pangbourne Wharf. Another Ashley had boat-houses for building and letting craft and even a slipway for servicing houseboats and steam launches. Several hotels in Pangbourne provided accommodation for 'river tourists', and also kept horses and carriages for those who wished to explore the countryside. The village even boasted a coffee house.

Pangbourne exemplifies the spread of subtopia into rural villages close to the railway system, perhaps reviving communities which had started to decline; lack of work on the land and newly acquired education were

Pangbourne Weir pool

just two of the factors which were driving young people to the towns and cities to seek employment in domestic service and factories. The crumbling tied cottages they would once have taken over were now sold and 'prettied up', or torn down and replaced with a commuter's villa. In 1910 Charles Harper took a wistful look back to halcyon days on this part of the rural Thames, not knowing that in four years' time the greater cataclysm of World War I would fall on the young men of those communities, leaving few to receive and pass on the memories, traditions and values of Old England.

That was the brave time, the golden age of the river, when, rather more than a generation ago, the discovery of the Thames as a holiday haunt was first made. The fine rapture of those early tourists, who, deserting the traditional seaside lounge for a cruise down along the placid bosom of the Thames, from Lechlade to Oxford, and from Oxford to Richmond, were (something after the 'Ancient Mariner' sort) the first to burst into these hitherto unknown reaches, can never be recaptured. The bloom has been brushed from off the peach by the rude hands of crowds of later visitors. The waterside inns, once so simple under their heavy beetling eaves of thatch, are now modish instead of modest: and Swiss and German waiters, clothed in deplorable reach-me-down dress-suits and lamentable English of the Whitechapel-atte-Bowe variety, have replaced the neat-handed – if heavy-footed – Phyllises, who were almost in the likeness of those who waited upon old Izaak Walton, two centuries and a quarter ago.

Today, along the margin of the Thames below Oxford, some expectant mercenary awaits at every slipway and landing-place the arrival of the frequent row-boat and the plenteous and easily earned tip; and the lawns of riparian villas on either hand exhibit a monotonous repetition of 'No Landing-Place', 'Private', and 'Trespassers Prosecuted' notices; while side-channels are not infrequently marked 'Private Backwater'.

All the villages immediately giving upon the stream have suffered an equally marked change, and have become uncharacteristic of their old selves, and converted into the likeness of no other villages in this our England, in these our times. There is, for example, a kind of theatrical prettiness and pettiness about Whitchurch, over against Pangbourne; and instead of looking upon it as a real, living 365-days-in-the-year kind of place, you are apt to think of what a pretty 'set' it makes; and, doing so, to speak of its bearings in other than the usual geographical terms of east and west, north and south; and to refer to them, indeed, after the fashion of the stage, as 'P.' or 'O.P.' sides.

But if we find at Whitchurch a meticulous neatness, a compact and small-scale prettiness eminently theatrical, what

The George Hotel landing-stage, Pangbourne

shall we say of its neighbour, Pangbourne, on the Berkshire bank of the river? That is of the other modern riverain type: an old village spoiled by the expansion that comes of being situated on a beautiful reach of the Thames, and with a railway station in its very midst. Detestable so-styled villas, and the kind of shops you find nowhere else than in these Thames-side spots, have wrought Pangbourne into something new and strange; and motor cars have put the final touch of sacrilege upon it.

Perhaps you would like to know of what type the typical Thames-side village shop may be, nowadays? Nothing easier than to draw its portrait in few words. It is, to begin with, inevitably a 'stores', and is obviously stocked with the first object of supplying boating-parties and campers with the necessaries of life, as understood by campers and boating-parties. As tinned provisions take a prominent place in those holiday commissariats, it follows that the shop-windows are

The Oxford Road and Shooter's Hill, Pangbourne, before Victorian development

almost completely furnished with supplies of tinned everything, festering in the sun. For the rest, you have cheap camp-kettles, spirit-stoves, tin enamelled cups and saucers, and the like utensils, hammocks and lounge-chairs.

Thus the modern riverside village is unpleasing to those who like to see places retain their old natural appearance, and dislike the modern fate that has given it a spurious activity in a boating-season of three months, with a deadly dull off-season of nine other months every year. We may make shift to not actively dislike these sophisticated places in summer, but let us not, if we value our peace of mind, seek to know them in winter; when the sloppy street is empty, even of dogs and cats; when rain patters like small-shot on the roof of the inevitable

tin-tabernacle that supplements the over-restored, and spoiled, parish church; and when the roar of the swollen weir fills the air with a thudding reverberance. Pah!

The villas, the 'maisonettes', are empty; the gardens draggle-tailed; the 'Nest' is 'To Let'; the 'Moorings' are 'To be Sold'; and a general air of 'has been' pervades the place, with a desolating feeling that 'will again be' is impossible.

But let us put these things behind us, and come to the river itself; to the foaming weir under the lowering sky, where such a head of water comes hurrying down that no summer frequenter of the river can ever see. There is no dead, hopeless season in nature; for although the trees may be bare, and the groves dismantled, the wintry woods have their own beauty, and even in mid-winter give promise of better times.

But along the uppermost Thames, from Thames Head to Lechlade and Oxford, the waterside villages are still very much what they have always been. All through the year they live their own life. Not there do the villas rise redundant, nor the old inns masquerade as hotels, nor chorus-girls inhabit at weekends, in imitative simplicity. A voyage along the thirty-two miles of narrow, winding river from Lechlade to Oxford has no incidents more exciting than the shooting of a weir, or the watching of a moor-hen and her brood.

Below Oxford, we have but to adventure some little way to right or left of the stream, and there, in the byways (for main roads do not often approach the higher reaches of the river) the unaltered villages abound.

As we approach Reading, A.J. Church, at a time when a Preservation Act was coming into force, illustrated in this region of the Thames the perennial conflict between the need for public access and recreation and, at the same time, the preservation of wildife. He justifiably condemned the anglers for the destruction of the otter, and

New villas known as 'The Seven Deadly Sins', Shooter's Hill

then, practically in the next breath, called for public footpaths and ferries to encourage walkers, which, by their very presence, would drive otters away. Later he even boasted of the hundreds of small defenceless fish he dragged from their natural element, purely for his pleasure.

Below Pangbourne the river valley opens out again, the meadows stretching in wide expanse, especially on the Berkshire shore. The river, too, which is curiously full of rushes and weed-beds, is, perhaps, less attractive than usual; but a walk of two miles, or thereabouts, will bring him [*the walker*] to what is, I venture to think, the most exquisite spot in its whole course, Mapledurham. Let him note on his way, first, on the Oxfordshire shore, Hardwick House, a picturesque building of some antiquity, the seat of the Powys family and an admirable specimen of the manor houses of southern England; and, secondly, four or five hundred yards above Mapledurham Lock,

Mapledurham Lock

a little wooded island. This I knew now more than forty years ago as the haunt of an otter, and it suggests a word of protest, useless I fear, as such words almost always are, against the barbarous Philistinism which is banishing, if it has not already banished, this beautiful creature from the Thames. It is ruthlessly trapped and shot because the angling societies grudge it its tribute out of the multitude of coarse fish with which, though they are increasingly difficult to catch, the river still abounds. I should gladly see the passing of an Act which would give an absolute protection to what may be still left of the once abundant *fauna* of the Thames, the otter, first of all, and with him too the kingfisher, the grebe, and the moorhen, now made the victims of useless massacre, 'butchered to make a Cockney's holiday'.

As I have come across the subject of what might be done by law to protect the beauties of the Thames, and make them as widely available as possible for the enjoyment of the public, I may take the opportunity of touching on one or two other points. For myself, and, I presume, others who knew and loved the river many years ago, the whole place is changed beyond all remedy. For in pleasure, as in business, 'all the markets overflow'; and thousands have found out the delights that were known to but a few here and there. . . .

On the Berkshire side of the river, Purley is noticeable for the beautiful variety of timber with which the park reaching down to the river – but, alas! cruelly bisected by the railway – is planted. Some of my pleasantest experiences of angling in days gone by are connected with the river at Mapledurham and the reaches below it, about half the way down to Reading. . . . Between thirty and forty years ago one of my brothers and myself used to make our headquarters for a week or so in the later summer at the Roebuck, a house which every frequenter of the Upper Thames will know. It is now a handsome hostelry, with spacious dining-saloons, a printed *menu*, a wine *carte* with some thirty vintages upon it at fashionable prices. The fact that one of the University crews made it their abode during a part of their preparation for the great race has given it an almost European celebrity. Nothing less can be said of a place which, for a time at least, furnished the papers with its quota of intelligence as regularly as did Paris or Egypt. In the days of which I speak it was nothing more than a roadside public house, deriving a little extra custom from occasional visitors who made their way thither by water from Reading. I remember that when we first proposed to take up our abode there for a week the idea seemed to strike our hostess as a surprising novelty; and, indeed, the accommodation – the

Caversham from the Reading meadows

quaint bedroom with its yellow-washed walls and low ceiling, and the narrow lattices, not too well used to opening – was of the most primitive kind. The old building still stands unchanged by the side of its fashionable successor; and dusty drovers on their way to Reading market rest, as of old, under the elms before the door; but the riverside inn as I knew it in my youth is no more. I must confess that our sport was of the humblest kind, nothing more than the gudgeon-fishing for which I have already ventured, *pace* those who follow the lordly arts of salmon and trout-fishing, or fill their creels with pike and perch, to offer an apology. But for gudgeon-fishing it was a very paradise. Near to Mapledurham itself the stream ran too rapidly for the purpose; but in the neighbourhood of the Roebuck there were spots that, as far as my experience goes, could not be rivalled elsewhere. In one place there would be fine sand, with some three or four feet of rather swift current over; in another a somewhat coarse gravel, with six or seven feet of slower water above, that was still more prolific. It was a delight which a summer day, aye, and a week of summer days, could not exhaust to move from one spot to another, and endeavour in the new locality to exceed the record of what had been achieved in the old. There was little question of size. The fish were curiously uniform in this respect, a peculiarity which is not uncommonly noticed by anglers in various branches of their sport. The commonest measure would be about four inches; a fish that reached to as much as six was almost a prodigy. But they made up in number what they wanted in magnitude. Our largest basket was *thirty-five dozen*, caught by two rods, without the help, it must be remembered, of a professional fisherman.

CHAPTER THREE

Reading to Maidenhead

The origins of the town of Reading are centred on the site of the great medieval abbey, which stood on the banks of the River Kennet some distance from its confluence with the Thames. During the nineteenth century the town had expanded at an incredible rate. The huge biscuit manufactory of Huntley and Palmer, the seed nurseries of Messrs. Sutton and Sons, ironworks, breweries, malthouses and factories, brought employment for thousands. But J.E. Vincent wrote in THE STORY OF THE THAMES, that this expansion gave the town a greater number of buildings distinguished by their uncompromising ugliness and endless streets of plain and staring redbrick houses. Even so, Victorian Reading hardly intruded upon the river view at Caversham. This was dominated, until 1869, by a great venerable bridge, some sections of which consisted of narrow medieval stone arches, much patched with brick. Halfway across, the bridge stood upon an island which once held the bridge chapel of St Anne. On the Reading side, the bridge was of wood, set on huge timber piles driven into the river bed. In 1869 the ancient structure was replaced by a functional iron girder bridge set on pairs of concrete-filled iron cylinders. This in turn was replaced by two elegant spans of concrete in 1926.

At the Berkshire end of the bridge, isolated in a broad expanse of lush meadows, stood the ancient White Hart inn, catering for barge as well as road-borne traffic. The inn was replaced at the beginning of the pleasure- boating boom by Bona's Caversham Bridge Hotel. Very soon, where flowered meadows had drifted down to the reedy water's edge, an orderly line of flood embankments appeared, to be followed by landing-stages, slipways and black and white 'Thames Tudor' commercial boat-houses. The firms of East, Moss, Freebody, Tims and Cawston established themselves on both sides of the river and on the central islands. Intrusive as these boat-houses may have seemed at the time, they appear perhaps beautiful now compared to the twentieth-century developments which have since dwarfed them.

Before we reach Kennet Mouth the broad reach is impounded by Caversham Weir, once a mill-dam holding back the current for the large

Caversham Lock

Bona's Caversham Bridge Hotel and boat-yards

mills at Lower Caversham, and, until 1778, when the pound lock was built, containing the usual flash lock. In 1884 the Conservancy replaced the old structure with a long series of iron sluice-gates. Twelve years later a new 'tumbling bay' was added. For some unknown reason the weir has long been known as The Clappers.

Below Caversham, once the railway has disappeared away to the right, we are back in the country again and approaching delightful Sonning. Like Streatley, the bridge, church and quaint houses drew Victorian artists by the score, some wealthy enough to stay in the waterside hotels, including, perhaps, Mortimer Menpes, who came here with writer G.E. Mitton, exploring for their joint venture THE THAMES, published in 1906.

Roses grow well all along by the river, but nowhere so well as they do at Sonning, and the rose garden forms an attraction which draws hundreds to the place. Yet Sonning has other attractions too; it is very varied and very pretty. When one arrives at it first, perhaps coming upstream, one is rather perplexed to discover the exact topography. We round a great curve which closes an osier bed; here, in early spring, the osiers may be seen lying in great bundles, shaded from olive-green to brown madder. Then we see some green lawns and landing places beneath the shadow of a fine clump of elms, and catch the sight of the lovable old red-brick bridge, with its high centre arch, spanning the stream. But there is another bridge, a wooden foot-bridge, which also spans the stream, at right angles to the other, and peeping through beneath this, we can see the continuation of the red-brick one in a new iron structure, which stretches on right up to the neat flower beds of the French Horn Hotel. The truth is, the river suddenly widens out here into a great bulge, and in the bulge are several islands, on one of which are a mill and a house and several other things, not to forget a charming garden. Above the bridge can be seen rising the little grey church tower. On one side is the White Hart Hotel, with its warm tone of yellow wash, its red tiles and creepers, and above all its famous rose garden. In the foreground is a willow-covered ait [*eyot*] placed in exactly the right position. But yet this is not the best side of the bridge. The other side is better; for here, to resist the flow of the current, the builders placed the buttresses which emphasize the height of that centre arch; buttresses now capped with tufty grass and emerald moss, and from the crevices of which spring clumps of yellow daisies, candytuft, wallflower, hart's-tongue fern, and other things. In the bricks all colours may be seen, after the manner of worn bricks, not even excluding blue. The mill is, as it should be, wooden, and is mentioned in Domesday Book. From the dark shadow beneath its wheel, the largest on the river, gurgles away the water in cool green streams, passing beneath

Thames Conservancy launch Loddon *in Sonning Lock*

the overhanging boughs of planes and horse-chestnuts. From the mighty sweep of the wheel, as it may be seen in its house, the drops rise glittering in cascades to varying heights like the sprays of diamonds on a tiara. The mill-house, called Aberlash, stands not far off on the same island, with a delightful garden.

This island spreads on with green lawns in a sweeping semi-circle to the lock and cottage, and from two small weirs the water dances down, adding variety to a beautiful pool where stand many irregular pollard willows on tiny aits. Over the smaller weir, framed in a setting of evergreens, is a bit of far distant blue landscape.

Sonning Bridge

From Sonning to Shiplake we begin to see the classic scenery of the Middle Thames; wooded hills rise in the distance on either side of the wide flood plain; alders and willows edge the broad, gently meandering stream. Rounding a bend, a clump of trees may suddenly appear, apparently floating in the middle of the channel, but set upon an eyot or island, bound together by the massed roots. Shiplake Lock is suddenly in front of us, perhaps not so noticeable after the landmark of the great weather-boarded mill beside it was pulled down in 1907. Prior to that, the mill and lock provided studies for many artists and photographers; even more so before 1874, when the century-old picturesque timber and turf-sided lock was replaced. The artist George Leslie appreciated the view, calling the mill a fine specimen 'having plenty of nice woodwork about it'; obviously completely uninterested in the work it had been

doing for centuries. He does comment on the little camping-parties who set up their tents on the lock island: this had long been a popular camp site and was specifically purchased for this purpose by the Corporation of London in 1889. Here, impoverished people from London's East End were sent for a week or so for a holiday in pure country air. The camp and bathing-place were strictly men-only. If the women-folk did come down to join them they were segregated on another island.

Shiplake, and its opposite neighbour, Wargrave, both provide excellent boat-houses and hotels for the weary oarsman; but we must press onward to Marsh Lock, to join George Leslie, as he shoves his punt towards Henley, for it is Regatta time. (Note that, as Leslie was going downstream, he should have said that the lock emptied, not filled!)

Marsh Lock is a terrible one to pass through on a Regatta morning. I shall never forget coming through from Wargrave on one of these occasions. The gates could hardly open on account of the jam of boats against them, everybody as usual wanting to get in first, the ladies being by far the most eager and energetic in their endeavours. The whole mass of boats shaped itself into the form of a huge arrow-head, and right down into the middle of the pack came slowly but surely a large tug-barge, called the *Spitfire* (since blown-up and wrecked at Sonning), with a crowd of Reading folks on board at a shilling a head. As the gates at last opened, the wedge tightened up, and I was glad to remember that my punt's sides were inch stuff, and the oak treads very strong, for I felt and heard the sides of other boats giving way like baskets, with many an ominous creak; outriggers and rowlocks got jammed and broken, and amidst cries and vituperation of every sort, the lock gradually filled. I had no idea how many boats a lock would really hold till then. The excitement reached its pitch when the gun at Henley was heard announcing the start of the first race, and the instant the

Shiplake Lock and Mill

lower gates could be opened the whole crowd of boats rushed out, splash, dash, and away, like school boys out of school.

The return from the Regatta is never so bad, as people leave the course at various hours, and no one is in any very great hurry, but the poor lock-keeper has a very hard day's work. . . .

The week before the races begin, Henley seems to wake up from its usual apathy; along the high roads boats on carts are seen continually arriving; various crews take up their quarters about the town, their respective flags hanging out from the upper windows. On the bridge from morn till night a constant string of idlers and rowing men lean on the balustrade, watching the practice or gossiping with each other. The time-honoured timbers of the Grand Stand are brought out and solemnly fixed

in their places. There is nothing very grand about this stand, for it is not unlike a large, broad, 'Punch and Judy' box.

On the day before the race, the scene becomes still more animated; a line of empty carriages is formed across the bridge on the side overlooking the course; a few gipsies, with Aunt Sallies and knock-'em-downs, come wandering up, whilst boats and boatmen from all parts of the river, gradually fill every available landing-place along the quays between the bridge and the railway station. Wherever camping is allowed, small tents are seen, with their picturesque inhabitants busy in cooking, and making themselves at home. Great houseboats and steam launches, one after another, are taking up their positions along the appointed line, which, gay with bunting, already stretches down towards Phillis Court. There are also numbers of small boats and punts with awnings rigged up in them, beneath which parties of two or three make themselves independent of lodgings in the town. The occupants of these boats, and the campers generally, affect picturesque and rather outlandish costumes. Frequently at this time, two or three of them are met with, on foraging expeditions up the town, carrying great stone jugs for beer, or baskets of potatoes and meat.

The bathing-place in the morning is crowded, and, indeed, the variety of costumes and characters that throng the tow-path, the bridge, and the streets, are quite peculiar to Henley at Regatta time.

Early in the morning of the first day's racing, the bells of the old church ring out in the most cheering way; boats arrive in numbers from both up and down the river. The very early trains bring down a large mixture of itinerant fruitsellers, niggers, organ-grinders, boatmen, and general riff-raff, along with some of the more eager and interested of the spectators. The later trains are reserved for the *élite*; at Paddington the crowd on the platform, for these trains, is never a disagreeable or formidable

Marsh Lock

Wargrave Ferry

down by the boat-houses; the various colours of the different rowing clubs assume large and distinct masses, as the birds of a feather flock together, and form into knots of uniformity. The umpire's boat is seen getting up steam – a long, rakish-looking craft, with no cabins or railings about it; a boat of reputed fabulous speed, since celebrated in connection with the sad disaster at Shepperton. The umpire's boat is not popular with the floating spectators, partly on account of the rocking about they get from its swell, and partly on account of its taking, throughout the day, various parties of ladies and gentlemen as passengers. To this latter practice I most strongly object. I do not know whether any charge is made for the trip, but even if the passage is free, there is great want of taste about thus crowding a boat which at best is only tolerated as a necessary evil, and in which none but the umpire and some Press representatives ought to be allowed to accompany the engine- driver and steerer. Mr Lord, on a paddle-wheel steamer belonging to the Thames Conservancy, is now seen busy in putting things to rights; seeing that the various large craft are moored in their proper line, and sometimes towing obstructive barges right up through the bridge, far off out of harm's way; indeed, throughout the day, Mr Lord has a very hard time of it, and I believe few are aware how much of the comfort and orderliness of the Regattas are due to his skill, energy, and good temper.

The river gradually gets covered with boats in every direction. Train after train arrives, and happy crowds come streaming along in front of River Terrace down to the boats, or off in search of the friends they expect to meet. Fortunate are those who find their boats or friends safely at the appointed place, and many are the anxious people seen searching in vain, surrounded and harassed by the speculative boatmen who have brought up for the occasion every sort of thing with oars that will float, which are to be hired for fabulous sums. The crowd about the Lion and on the bridge now gets very dense. Boats on

one to mix in; the trains are well-managed, run frequently, and if only the sun shines, all are smiling and happy. From the windows of the train as it passes over the bridge at Shiplake, you may catch sight of numerous boat-loads, wending their way along downstream, and sometimes of one of those huge barges from Reading, with crowds of people standing on the deck. About ten o'clock a large waggonette, carrying the Eton boys, passes along the road in front of my mother's cottage; they all look very serious, and as old and manly as they possibly can. Racing ships and outriggers are now being lifted about carefully

Houseboats at Henley

Henley Regatta

the water are scattered about in apparently hopeless confusion, and presently the crew of an eight is seen to embark for the first heat of the Grand Challenge. They are slowly turned above the bridge, and paddling down through the arches they pass on, picking their way along the course, with frequent stops, to the starting point. They are very quickly followed by their antagonists, and the umpire's boat with warning whistle steams slowly down to the island; but still the crowd of floating spectators seems in hopeless confusion. The Conservancy men, with red flags in their boats, go to work in earnest, whilst gradually the floating masses sort themselves together, and range alongside of the moored houseboats and launches. Still, as each train arrives, or as a fresh batch of boats escapes through Marsh Lock, more and more happy boatfuls come straggling down onto the course, when bang goes the gun for the start, and with redoubled energy the Conservancy men row up the stream, clearing the water as they go, and gradually driving, like sheep dogs, the straying herds of boats towards the Oxford shore.

Nothing much is seen of the two eights at first; the umpire's steamer and the thick bunch of runners along the tow-path alone indicate their whereabouts. But in the meantime all sorts of opinions are freely given as to the probable results of the race; how it is a certainty for one on account of the station, or else that the shelter of the willows which favours the Bucks side will more than compensate for the advantages of the other shore, and in consequence we shall see a 'rattling good race'. Those of the spectators who have field-glasses begin very soon to declare which boat is leading, but much reliance can seldom be placed on these remarks, as it is impossible with three-quarters of a mile of foreshortening perspective, to judge correctly of a few yards' lead. It is not long, however, before the shouts from the runners on the banks grow more and more audible, and are

taken up by the spectators in the boats on the other side; in a few seconds more, two long lines of straining bodies dart past, the boats themselves seeming to lift and bound at each stroke in regular cadence. The race is generally pretty well decided as Phillis Court is passed, as anything like a lead here is seldom again lost. Amidst the roar of cheers and the swell from the umpire's boat the sound of the band is heard playing the well-known air, and the first heat is lost and won.

During past Ice Ages the combined forces of the Thames and Kennet rivers cut a wide valley deep into the southern flank of the Chiltern Hills, leaving an outlying range of high chalk country on the right hand from Wargrave to Cookham. The most impressive features of this range, seen from the river, are the steep scarps at Remenham Hill, Henley, and Winter Hill, Cookham. The beech-clad slopes to the north of the river are interspaced with wide, predominantly dry, valleys sweeping down to the flood plain. They contain remote villages, built of chalk, flint and brick; before the coming of the motor car hardly touched by time. The villagers had at least one windmill to grind their corn, but no watermills, because any streams in this high country were little more than winterbournes, with channels only containing water during wet seasons. Therefore the great Thames mills at Marsh, Hambleden, Hurley and Marlow were important to communities far from the river, well into Victorian times. At Aston and Medmenham, where the towing-path changes sides, ancient ferries existed: Medmenham Ferry was indubitably founded by the adjacent riverside abbey, which, after its partial destruction at the Dissolution, became the eighteenth-century headquarters of the notorious Hellfire Club. Later, a country house was built within the standing ruins, which became part residence, part folly. During alterations in about 1865, the head workman was asked what they were doing: 'We're renovating the old place, Sir — making it look more ancient like.'

Downstream at Danesfield, the chalky hills end abruptly at the river as a perpendicular white cliff, on top of which sit the ramparts of an Iron

A Thames Conservancy launch and rowing eights at Henley

Hambleden Lock

Age hill fort, nothing whatsoever to do with Danes. Just below, Hurley Weir was New Lock in the sixteenth century and still called 'New Lock' in Victorian times. Henry Taunt, in rare artistic mood, wrote lovingly of Harleyford, below the weir. Alas, the 'lovely wooded bits' have been desecrated in the name of profitable pleasure. Harleyford House, the best contender for Kenneth Grahame's 'Toad Hall', and surely the worst of Sir Robert Taylor's architectural efforts, sits uncomfortably in ultra-modern surroundings.

Passing down from Medmenham a group of islands is soon reached, beautifully decorated in the autumn with white water-lilies in the eddies, and purple loosestrife, as well as numerous other waterside plants round the banks; a little lower, numerous beds of reeds cover over the sides of the stream with their luxurious growth, standing up from the river several feet in height. And now begins a bold range of chalk cliffs, partially covered with foliage, and the river widens out into a clear lake-

Medmenham Ferry

New Lock Weir, Hurley

like piece of water till New Lock weir is reached. When nearing the overfall *keep closely to the right hand towing-path bank,* at all events in high water-time, *as the weir directly faces the centre of the stream,* and the draught from it is very great at times. The river at New Lock is sweetly pretty, and more than one picture is seen where the white chalk cliffs, with their relieving foliage, act as a foil to the rushing water of the weir. Through the open part of the weir, and down the back water, was the navigable waterway in olden times; and close to the cottages stands the old capstan, which was then used to force the barges up the fall against the rush of the stream. In the backwater are some lovely wooded bits for the artist, the old dilapidated eel bucks, with their stage of broken woodwork, and the river plants springing up around the base of the piles on which they stand; here and

there a tree partly down across a stream, and leaning its weight on others, whilst, out of the dense foliage, the swift flying kingfisher darts like a flash of coloured lightning as he skims over the sparkling water beneath. Harleyford House, the seat of Sir William Clayton, stands just below, sheltered behind by its beautiful hanging woods.

Within a mile of Hurley we are at Temple Lock, and, if we are rowing or punting, after 1890, perhaps we bypass the lock by using the slipway and rollers which, because of the large numbers of small craft available for hire at Marlow, the Conservancy thoughtfully installed. To the right, behind the long overfall weir and islands, stand the impressive brick buildings and chimneys of Temple Paper Mill. Above the sound of the mill races, the beating of huge water wheels and pulping machinery can be heard. Next on the right, in total contrast, the mellowed brick, flint and chalk of the house and barns of Bisham Abbey form a perfect grouping near the edge of the reed-fringed river. Close at hand, the same local building materials are reflected in the water below the Norman tower of Bisham Church.

James Thorne was not very impressed with the 'second-rate agricultural town' of Marlow, when he rambled through it in 1847.

It has a good many shops, but they are mostly small and of a common-place kind. It has several inns, and one a very tolerable one. . . . The handsome suspension bridge was erected in 1835, and is a great ornament to the river. The church stands at the foot of the bridge, and was built about the same time. It is of the style fitly named 'modern Gothic', and is, with infinite good nature, greatly admired by the inhabitants – who do not, however, so much admire the tax laid on them for bridge and church . . . There is an annual cattle-fair, at which there is generally a great show of horses, and usually some of the large size and excellent form are exhibited . . . The pleasure-fair

Harleyford House

seems a dull one. The countrymen hereabout are not of a mirthfull cast, and their liveliness is of a very laborious character. . . . I am afraid that Marlow has still a very poor population. The houses about the meaner streets have a wretched poverty-stricken aspect, and there are more evident signs of vice forcing themselves on the attention than is at all common in country-towns of the same size and class. And the complaints of the inhabitants accord fully with the general appearance.

The waterfront at Marlow, like Henley, at one time held wharves and warehouses busy with barge traffic to and from London, but which had greatly declined in the first half of the century, partly because of competition from the railway. However, in 1868 local businessmen promoted the Great Marlow Railway Company to bring a three-mile branch line along the riverside from Bourne End, which was on the Maidenhead to High Wycombe line. It was opened with great rejoicing in 1873 and helped to revitalize the town. Leisure-boating proprietors

Shoal dredging at Hurley Lock

were already established at abandoned wharves by the bridge: Robert Shaw and Haynes and Son were both advertising in THE ROWING ALMANACK in 1862. Meakes and Redknap established themselves on the Berkshire bank not long afterwards. Marlow Regatta never became as fashionable as Henley but the railway brought large numbers of pleasure-seekers for boating, camping and fishing: a total of nine professional fishermen are listed in Taunt's Guide. The town hotels expanded for the trade, including the old Anglers inn by the weir, whose landlord gave it an up-market image by stealing the title of the seventeenth-century Izaak Walton's literary gem THE COMPLETE ANGLER. Only later was it given the original 'Compleat' spelling, to attract the American tourists.

After passing Little Marlow, James Thorne saw hardly a house on the riverside, only 'a succession of sweet bits of river scenery', until Hedsor. The sprawling village of Bourne End did not exist then; it began with the establishment of the railway station and was first called Marlow Road. The line from Maidenhead initially crossed the river on a wooden trestle bridge, later replaced by one of iron. The lovely open Bourne End Reach, set in a natural bowl rimmed by Winter Hill and the beech-capped Chilterns, became a famous sailing course, with weekend races and annual regattas organized by the Upper Thames Sailing Club. Messrs Horsham and Company established a boatyard at an old wharf near the station and advertised as steam-launch, yacht, houseboat and boat builders. Their steamer Alaska, built as a private launch, was one of the first to be acquired by Salter Brothers for the Oxford to Kingston run. A century later she was found as a derelict hulk and lovingly restored to her former glory.

At Cookham, a short distance hence on the Berkshire shore, the pretty village fared the same as all the others on the Middle Thames, being shaken out of its slow rural existence by brash visitors from London. The ancient Ferry Inn, by the side of a comparatively new wooden, and later iron toll-bridge, was given a Victorian façade towards the river and renamed Llewellyn's Hotel. The proprietor also established a boat-hire and sales business, competing with William Lacey, also by the bridge.

Downstream, the river splits into four separate channels; combining again as one under the spectacular woods of Cliveden. The left hand was the original navigation channel, flowing past ancient Hedsor Wharf. It was blocked by a weir after the next channel, Cookham Lock Cut, was opened in 1830. On the right hand is the mill stream to Cookham Paper Mill. The intervening channel leads to Odney Weir and Pool, the subject of a locally famous court case in 1876. A lady had extended the grounds of her house by enclosing part of the village Common Land at Odney, and was so shocked when she saw youths bathing naked in the pool above the weir, that she had six of them

Marlow Regatta

Marlow Mills and Weir from the church tower, with Quarry Woods and Winter Hill beyond

prosecuted for indecency. The village immediately rallied to collect cash for a Cookham Bathing and Boating Defence Fund, to fight the lads' case and defend the usual practice of all classes to bathe in this quiet backwater as they wished. With no running water in many village houses at this time, river bathing was more a means of getting clean rather than of recreation. The Fund obtained enough finance, with the active support of Baronet Sir George Young who resided at nearby Formosa Island, to brief a top defence counsel, who made a successful

plea of 'Not Guilty'. The case gained much publicity and did much to promote swimming at Odney; a club was formed and annual contests staged. Maidenhead Swimming Club also held annual long-distance races along Cliveden Reach, starting at Cookham Lock.

Maidenhead, or correctly, nearby Taplow, was the first Thames-side place to be influenced by the Great Western Railway, but perhaps we can also partly blame Mr and Mrs Hall for its subsequent popularity. When they passed through taking notes for THE BOOK OF THE THAMES, the river view contained Brunel's magnificent new railway bridge, the toll-bridge carrying the Great West Road, the Orkney Arms (later Skindles Hotel), the weir and lock, Ray corn mills and Taplow paper mill, and little else except osier-clad islands, eel-traps, open fields and meadows: Maidenhead itself was set back on rising ground some distance away.

In this district, indeed, are to be found all the several advantages which the noble river so abundantly supplies: a channel of depth sufficient for any required traffic, a populous and flourishing town close at hand, pleasant cottages, comfortable inns, and villas, grand or graceful, scattered at convenient intervals, by the banksides, on the slopes of adjacent elevations,

or crowning distant hills in the midst of 'patrician trees' and 'plebeian underwood'; while the heart-cheering turrets of Windsor Castle occasionally come in sight, to add to the interest of the scenery the lessons and pleasures of association. The land is thus fertile in themes, and the water is hardly less so: the barges, the punts, the gay wherries, the racing boats are everywhere; and perhaps in no part of the world are there to be obtained enjoyments so many or so full – at once so quiet and so active – as are to be found in this part of the Thames, where the venerable Father leads us to classic Eton and regal Windsor.

Thirty years later Taunt observed that the riverside at Ray Mead had grown very fashionable within a few years; the road being dotted with villa residences. Private clubs appeared among the villas, including the famous Guards Club. Two new hotels were also built on the bank; both ran several steam launches and had small craft for hire. The boat builder Jonathan Bond was in business by the bridge before 1862, and later built an impressive series of steam launches. Harry Wilder and H. and S. Rose also had premises for building small boats. At the Ray Mead Hotel there were even ponies for hire for towing craft along the river. (It had become common practice to walk along the bank with a towing line connected to a short mast on the boat, with someone steering, particularly against a strong wind or current; hiring a pony with a handler was the ultimate luxury.)

At the height of the season, particularly the Sunday of Royal Ascot Week, up to eight hundred boats had been known to pass through Boulter's Lock in one day, not to go anywhere in particular, but just to be seen at one of the most fashionable places in the whole of the Empire. The innumerable paintings, photographs and postcards of Boulter's can record the visual impact of a busy day, but to gather some impression of the excitement of being there in person, we need the Pennells, still on their STREAM OF PLEASURE.

Beneath Quarry Woods

My Lady *Ferry, Cliveden*

Beneath the steep wooded slopes of Cliefden – where here and there the cedars and beeches leave a space to show the great house of the Duke of Westminster rising far above, its gray façade in fine perspective against the sky – up the near backwaters winding between sedge and willow, one to a mill, another to a row of eel butts, the number of the smaller boats was legion. Among them was every possible kind of row-boat, and there were punts, some with one, some with two at the pole, dinghies, sail-boats, even a gondola and two sandolas, and canoes with single paddle, canoes with double paddles, and one at least with an entire family on their knees paddling as if from the wilds of America or Africa. On the Thames it seems as if no man were too old, no child too young, to take a paddle, a pole, or a scull. In one boat you find a grey-haired grandfather, in the next a little girl in short frocks and big sun-bonnet.

The locks were more crowded than usual, and on their banks

William Deacon's launch Wild Rose *at Ray Mead Hotel, Maidenhead*

men waited with baskets of fruit and flowers. In one we sunk to the bottom to the music of the 'Brave General', and the musicians, when there was no escape, let down the lock-keeper's boat-hook with a bag at the end for pennies.

But it was outside Boulter's Lock, on the way back to Cookham, that we found the greatest crowd. There were such a mass of boats one might have thought all . . .

> The men who haunt the waters,
> Broad of breast and brown of hue,
> All of Beauty's youngest daughters,
> Perched in punt or crank canoe

. . . were waiting to pass through together. But presently the lock-keeper called out, 'Keep back! There are a lot of boats coming!' and the lock gates slowly opened and out they came, pell-mell, pushing, paddling, poling, steaming and there was great scrambling, and bumping, and meeting of friends, and cries of 'How are you?' 'Come to dinner at eight,' 'Look out where you're going!' and brandishing of boat-hooks, and glaring of eyes, and savage shoutings, and frantic handshakings, and scrunching of boats, and scratching of paint, and somehow we all made our way into the lock as best we could, the lock-keeper helping the slower boats with his long boat-hook and fitting all in, until there was not space for one to capsize if it would. But indeed in a crowded lock if you cannot manage your own boat someone else will manage it for you; and, for that matter, when there is no crowd you meet men whose only use of a boat-hook is to dig it into your boat as you are quietly making your way out. Both banks were lined with people looking on, for Boulter's Lock on Sunday afternoon is one of the sights of the Thames.

When the upper gates opened, there was again pushing and scrambling, and it was not until we were out of the long cut and under the Cliefden heights that we could pull with ease. The

Cookham Lock

boats kept passing long after we had got back to Cookham and while we lingered in the hotel garden. Almost the last were the sandolas and the gondola, and as we watched them, with the white figures of the men at the oar outlined against the pale sky and bending in slow, rhythmic motion, we understood why these boats are so much more picturesque than the punt, the action of the gondolier so much finer than that of the punter. The entire figure rises above the boat, and there is no pause in the rhythm of the motion. In a punt the man at the pole, except in the upper reaches near Oxford, stands not above but in the boat; and fine as is his action when he draws the pole from the water and plunges it in again, the interval when he pushes on it or walks with it is not so graceful. To know the punt at its very best you should see it in a race, when the action of the punter is as continuous as that of the gondolier.

Cliveden Reach

The gondola the Pennells saw, on its way back home after satisfactorily completing its part in the game of one-upmanship at Boulter's Lock, was indubitably that owned by Mr C. Hammersley of the large riverside residence of Abney House, Bourne End. Slaving at its single oar on the upstream voyage was Giulio, reputed to be a genuine gondolier. The craft was a well-known visitor to social events and regattas, including, of course, Henley.

Cliveden Reach must then have been a paradise for nature lovers and pleasure-boaters. Even in the eighteenth century it was a place for outdoor social activities; the local gentry and their ladies picnicking in the glades by Cliveden Spring, which still has its outlet close to the river. The hanging woods on the heights of Cliveden and Taplow, described in glowing terms by so many writers, have stood the test of time remarkably well: the river has not been so fortunate. Victorian photographs illustrate that the multitude of small craft described by the Pennells, drifted along a delightful river, shallower than today, amid a

profusion of water plants reaching out from either bank; the osier covered eyots protected with massed reeds and rushes. Now the river's gravel bed, and even the chalk rock below it, has been dredged to deepen it for flood alleviation and navigation, and the waves from fast motor craft strip away any plant that has the temerity to try to colonize the shore.

Most of the boats passing through Boulter's Lock were hired craft, and, as there is little difference between one skiff or punt, and the next, one of the few ways of showing one's social status was in the manner of fashion. The dressmaking and millinery industry boomed as Victorian and Edwardian ladies went to extraordinary lengths to be in the season's fashion; even the less well-off girl, being well-instructed with the needle, would make something special for river outings, in case she met that certain someone. G.E. Mitton seems to have gone quite overboard describing the enticing sights of the fashion parade at Boulter's.

Human beings are by nature sociable; and to state that a crowd of well-dressed people will be at a certain point of the river at a particular date, is to ensure that everyone else who possibly can will be there too – only better dressed. It would seem to the ordinary ungregarious bachelor that Boulter's Lock, the Sunday after Ascot, would be a place to avoid, for there will be the necessity of waiting for hours on a river – grilling in the sun if the day be fine, or shivering if the day be cloudy; for the English climate never lacks the spice of uncertainty, and at this season of the year it is more capricious than usual. The middle of June is proverbially a time of roses, but it is just as likely to be a time for chills, at least so says the pessimist. To the optimist and he who 'loves his fellow-men', Boulter's Lock, on this one day of the year, reveals itself to memory as a day of delight and flashing colour; he has only to shut his eyes to recall a scene as brilliant as a flower garden. Here, close to him, lies a long, flat-bottomed punt, with gay cushions on which lean two fair girls, their faces toned to a pink glow by the sun's rays penetrating gently

Boulter's Lock, Maidenhead

through their rose-pink sunshades. Their large flapping hats are tied under their chins with huge bows of ribbon as pink as their cheeks; their soft, white muslin dresses lie in folds and frills and heaps bewildering to contemplate; they are exactly, exasperatingly, absurdly alike. 'How can a woman be such an idiot as to duplicate her charms?' the onlooker exclaims to himself; but he looks again. Dark eyes dancing as merrily as the ripples on the breeze-stirred water; chatter and laugh; and babble as soft and meaningless as the gurgle of the little tributary stream; textures of fabric as delicate as the flowers peeping over the grey stone walls from the lock-keeper's garden above; dainty arms bare to the elbow; Japanese umbrellas jewelled in the sunlight; striped awnings, as gay as Joseph's coat, flapping softly; the long low outlines of craft of every kind, skiff and dingey and canoe, from the smoothly gliding little electric launch to the heavy clinker-built boat on hire for its tenth season; these items make up a scene quite unlike anything else. For half a mile below the lock you could step across a solid bridge of boats over half the river. Some years ago, the homely serge and sailor straw-hat was considered the proper river costume; now, the straw is worn only by men, whose severe flannels show little alteration from year to year, for men are much more conservative in sartorial matters than women. And every tantalizing muslin, lace, and flower-decked hat is considered suitable for a woman on the river. The more fantastic and enormous, the more gauzy and lace-trimmed, the better. And, as her grandmother did, the young girl dresses in the thinnest of muslins and lawns, wears an open neck in the day time, and elbow sleeves.

In pushing forward between the open lock-gates into the lock, a slender canoe fits into an almost impossible space between the electric launch and the punt. A heavily weighted boatload, where four elderly women are rowed by one heated man, falls foul of its neighbour and has to be righted. The chatter is silenced for a moment, but rises again when the craft are fitted, like the pieces in an old-fashioned puzzle, inside the

Brunel's Great Western Railway Bridge, Taplow

green and slimy walls, which throw a deep shadow on one side. Then the gates are shut, and a wash and gurgle of water begins, delightfully cool to hear. A nervous girl gives a little shriek and jumps so that every boat is set a-rocking, as all are touching. Others laugh. It is impossible to upset, for there is no room. The whole gently swaying mass rises on the breast of the rising water up out of the shadow into the sunlight; into the view of the waiting crowds on the tow-path. Colours flash out once more; an excited little dog rushes yapping from stem to stern of his boat, and finally, with a vigorous jump, lands on the lock-keeper's garden, where there is a profusion of sweet old-fashioned flowers, and such roses as grow nowhere but by the riverside. Then, to the accompaniment of the dog's frantic barks, the massive gates creak backward on their hinges, and we ride forward into the wide expanse of the sparkling river.

CHAPTER FOUR

Maidenhead to Teddington

Turning about again, on our journey downstream, we pass under the road and rail bridges and onto the wide Bray Reach. As the heights of Taplow drop away behind us, we find that the character of the river changes, for we are leaving the Middle Thames Valley. Except where it is flanked by high ground at Windsor and Runnymede, the river now flows through a much wider expanse of flood-plain gravels, stretching away towards London. The reasonably straight Bray Reach made an ideal course for the popular Maidenhead regattas, both rowing and punting, especially after about 1889, when an obstructive eyot and redundant eel bucks were dredged away. The days of the big autumn eel migrations had long since gone, and many of the ancient traps were suffering the same fate. However, in George Leslie's day the picturesque structure at Bray was still standing.

After passing the railway-bridge there is nothing at all remarkable on the river until you near Bray; here the river takes a bend to the left, and on the right you pass an eyot with eel-bucks on one side of it. These eel-bucks are always picturesque things, and I may as well here say a few words about them. They are placed generally in backwaters out of the course of the regular navigation, in parts where the stream runs very sharply; a stage is raised up like a little wooden bridge, on the downstream side of which a set of square frames like gallows is erected: up these frames the eel-baskets are raised by small wooden windlasses. When the baskets are up, there is just room

for a boat to pass through the square opening underneath; all the passages of water above are fenced off, so that the fish are forced to go through the bucks on their way down, the back-water becoming a sort of funnel, with baskets as strainers at the end of it. There is often a small passage at the side, through which a boat can get past the bucks, but it is made so that you have to turn a short way up stream in order to go through; the

Rebuilding Bray Weir

The eel bucks at Bray

fish, of course, do not think of this back turn, as they pass along down stream.

On account of the old worn-out bucks, and the fencing and staking connected with them, all backwaters, if the water is not well known, should be passed with caution, as very dangerous snags and stumps may be met with, striking on which would be quite sufficient to knock a hole in a thin boat. In punting, as you look down so much into the water, they are generally perceived; a

punt's floor is, besides, strong enough to resist a good bump.

Below the bucks the vicarage, with the church behind it, form a charming group, and at the ferry is the George Hotel, where my punt was built when Woodhouse lived there.

Bray pound lock was the last to be built on the Lower Thames, not opening until 1845. It was at first a timber-built, turf-sided lock, with very little fall, provided by a long paddle and rymer weir, typical of the

Bray village

early weirs on the lower river. Both lock and weir were reconstructed forty years later. Through the lock, we drift down Dorney Reach, past Monkey Island Hotel, a favourite watering hole for royalty and gentry in the Edwardian Age, for now the area comes under the influence of Windsor and its Castle, its crag-like walls standing sentinel high above the winding river. At Boveney Lock we meet John Leyland, author of THE THAMES ILLUSTRATED.

About us, on either bank, are the greenest of meadows, and in places great beds of reeds and osiers, and there are boats going to and fro, houseboats, too, gay with flowers, and boatmen encamped by the shore. Regal swans have their nests among the reeds by the eyots and along the banks. They are a royal possession, and it once cost a year's imprisonment to steal a single egg; but royal favour long ago allowed them to the Dyers' and the Vintners' Companies. The work of swan-upping in July or August falls to the royal and other swan-herds. They cut the upper mandibles of the beautiful birds in a particular fashion to mark their ownership – a fashion a good deal modified since the Society for the Prevention of Cruelty to Animals expressed its displeasure at that which formerly prevailed. It is certainly a stirring and bustling sight, accompanied by much splashing of water, when the swan-herds proceed to their work.

We presently come to Boveney Lock, and, as the gates open, a promiscuous crowd of row boats, dinghies, punts and even sometimes, it may be, a gondola or two, come out with much flourishing of boat-hooks and oars, and many a cry of, 'Look where you're going!' as all go Windsor-ward. There was an ancient fishery at Boveney, and there is still a quaint little church to be visited. A very short distance above the lock in our upward journeying we come to Surly Hall – that riverside hostelry so dear to all Etonians, and the place, to which the college boats make their pilgrimage on the great aquatic festivals

Boveney Lock

of the College, occasions on which great havoc, they say, is wrought among the ducks and green peas.

From Boveney we begin to obtain the first clear views of Windsor Castle, which, as we approach, dominates the skyline. On the right, some of the town buildings of Windsor appear from behind a string of osier-clad islands; while to the left the cramped High Street houses of Eton lie beyond the broad Brocas meadow. The towns converge on either side of the river and are connected by a road bridge of three cast-iron arches. On either side are small boat-hire establishments, but otherwise the river frontage is dominated by the boat-houses and rafts of Eton College. There is a very long tradition of boating at the College, much of it social and ceremonial rather than competitive, and as is common within such an enclosed society, a number of strange customs evolved to support it, such as the duck-and-green-peas riverside suppers

The Eton Fourth of June celebrations

to which John Leyland alluded. The premier annual river event became the colourful pageant of the Fourth of June, celebrating the birthday of the College's benefactor, King George III. J.E. Vincent continues the description of the river at Eton in THE STORY OF THE THAMES.

We re-embark above Windsor Bridge, and passing under it, follow the right or Berkshire bank at the point where the river is divided into three branches. That on the left, which is narrow, washes the fellows' private portion of the Eton playing fields, and is private. It and the central stream (the broadest of the three, but it is barred by a weir) combine to make Fellows' Eyot where, on the annual and 'glorious' Fourth of June, the set pieces of fireworks are erected and displayed; that on the right, with the aid of a short 'cut' excavated in 1797, leads to the lock, rebuilt in 1869 and not in quite the same place as the original lock, which was, of course, contemporary with the 'cut'. From this reticulation of streams, and from the existence of the weir, come several consequences; the first of them being that the river, as it passes along the Eton playing fields, is to all intents and purposes private. Yet it is not on this part of the river, as men might think who did not know it, that Etonian oarsmen and watermen are made. In truth it is far too sinuous for hard rowing, and all the serious business of rowing – very grave indeed it can be – is done above the bridge. Only on the evening of the Fourth of June does the celebrated procession of boats, including the ten-oared *Monarch*, invade these waters, rowing first in gay state downstream to a point in Windsor Home Park where, Surley Hall being of the past, supper is provided, and then back to show real skill of watermanship in front of blazing fireworks. There are few more fascinating and exhilarating spectacles than this when the tawny fireworks, always including a piece showing 'Floreat Etona', cast flickering

Romney Lock, Windsor

gleams of gold upon the water, when their lurid smoke is a veil over all things in the background, when the crews of the light craft, garlanded with flowers as to their straw hats, in the uniform of the naval seaman of many years ago – the coxswains are executive officers – stand upright with oars raised, as if their boats equalled a man-of-war's cutter in steadiness. And if, now and again, a boat is capsized, nobody cares and all are the merrier, but without a shade of anxiety; for at Eton no boy may enter a boat until he has passed a fairly severe test in swimming. To the Colonial born, to the American, or to the foreign visitor to England, this annual river-festival may justly be recommended as showing young England in high spirits and at its best. The rest of the proceedings of the Fourth of June, being in the main esoteric in their interest, would probably be found tedious by a total stranger; but the words 'total stranger' must by no means be taken to cover all the Englishmen of other public schools and their relatives.

We avoid dangerous Romney Weir by passing through the lock cut to the right of the long extension to Romney Island known as the Cobbler. Through the lock the river makes a two-mile loop around the vast expanse of the Home Park, passing the village of Datchet to the left on the way. At the boundary of the park, not long before we pass down a long artificial cut, and through Old Windsor Lock, stands Albert Bridge, below described by Godfrey Turner in THE ROYAL RIVER. However, the bridge quickly becomes an excuse for Turner, obviously a rowing man, to air his not unexpected views on steam launches. Within a short distance of Old Windsor, and approaching historic Runnymede he is in a much better frame of mind, for where the main road converges on the river stands the Bells of Ouseley inn, which he found very much to his taste.

The Albert Bridge, Datchet

Albert Bridge, with its long, flattened, Tudor arch, spanning the river at one bound, bears a miniature resemblance to the design of the bridge at Westminster, and is light and elegant, though of a modern taste, which lacks the picturesqueness and simplicity of the old objects on the river. The span, however, adds safely to the navigation, especially in these times of steam launches, the most unpopular and best-hated craft on the Thames. Like other ills, we have come to tolerate them for a certain one-sided convenience, esteemed by the selfish, the lazy, and the fast. All pleasant quiet on the river, as, indeed, on the shore, is a thing of long ago. Idlesse, dreamy solitude, *could* only be enjoyed by the few, and *can* never be enjoyed by them. In coupling, or rather in

identifying the fast and the lazy, we may, by hasty thinkers, be suspected of a contradiction. There is none in what we have said. The lazy are often restless in their inert desire to be conveyed swiftly from place to place; for they have no energy for idling. To rush, screaming on, with their hands in their pockets, and no motion of their own, is the height of bliss to such people, and this is the enjoyment a steam launch affords. Yet the unpopular vessel has a popularity of its own. Riverside folk in the mass, from the Duke of Westminster to the poorest toiler who profits by the Early-closing Movement and the Bank-holidays, all join in decrying the rowdy intruder – the

The Bells of Ouseley Inn

''arry' of river craft. But ''arry' is all-pervading, and multiplies himself with astonishing exuberance and rapidity. There is more of him every day; and there are more and more steam launches, for all the outcry against them . . .

No traveller bids farewell to Old Windsor without paying his respects to one of the best of the riverside taverns, the time-honoured Bells of Ouseley. Perfectly free, at present, from modern revivalism, and from all manner of conscious style, is this genuine old inn, separated by the high road from the river bank. Its quaint bow-windows, one on either side of a porch entered by way of a steep flight of steps – the wholesome dread of unsteady topers – are just of the period and fashion to captivate an artist in search of the picturesque; nor can we look on this unspoilt hostelry without thinking of Mr Leslie, Mr Boughton, or Mr Tissot. In France, a village cabaret or auberge, humbler than this, would yet be far more advanced in the art of public entertainment. 'They cook very well at these places,' is a remark you frequently hear in Normandy, Picardy, or Champagne, from the lips of culinary judges, versed in all the intricacies of Parisian gastronomy; and if the unpretending inn be near a trout-stream, be sure you may have a dish fit for a prince, and within the means of a woodcutter. Were some enterprising cook to lease a cosy tavern like the Bells of Ouseley, and introduce a really high-class *cuisine* on a choice but simple scale, the place would be talked about in a month and spoiled in a year, at the end of which time the proprietor might be either a rich man or a bankrupt. Let us take our pretty, rustic riverside resort, for rest and refreshment, as we find it. Fine cookery would drive out honest companions whom old Izaak – who had a face like an elderly pike, but was a right good fellow for all that – would have drawn into profitable talk; for at the Bells of Ouseley you meet anglers and bargemen from whom much is to be learnt, if you go the right way to get hold of them. On the left as you enter is the tap, often crowded; on the right a bar-parlour, in which the company is more select. Of old the Bells had the reputation of being a house of call for 'minions of the moon', as Falstaff called them, or 'knights of the road', to choose a later phrase, such as the authors of *Paul Clifford* and *Rookwood* would have applied to the same order of gentry. But the landlord does not, in these days, give stall and fodder to nags of suspicious character, like bonny Black Bess. The old stone stable is oftener occupied by steeds that consume neither oats nor hay; and the highwaymen are not such as wear crape over their faces, or carry pistols like demi-culverins, or dance minuets with ladies they have plundered, but are in fact only members of a bicycle club. Under that old roof with its odd chimneys, standing against a background of greenery, there are jolly ghosts, you may be sure; for the grimmer goblins that have haunted the Bells in time when gibbets were plentiful, and when every one of these evil trees bore its rotting fruit, that swung and creaked in the night-wind, were laid long ago in a red sea of steaming punch, by boon companions of those who, as the phrase was, 'suffered'. The fishing at the Bells is good. Capital chub and dace are taken with the fly, and gudgeon are plentiful as blackberries.

Past the favoured picnic spots of Magna Carta Island and Ankerwyke and through Bell Weir Lock we arrive at Staines, described by Taunt as 'a quiet little town, very clean and bright'. However, ugly gasworks and road and rail bridges had already spoilt the view from the river, which now seems to cringe beneath even greater twentieth-century vandalism. The Victorian waterside had the usual complement of hotels and boat-houses for the river tourist, including the launch works of E. Burgoine and the boat-house of John Tims, close to the railway bridge; the latter having set up on his own after leaving Salter's of Oxford.

On the north bank, at the boundary between the counties of Buckinghamshire and Middlesex stands the thirteenth-century London Stone, marking the limit of the City of London's jurisdiction over the river. Here the Londoner's Thames begins in earnest; the Victorian railway's tentacles had spread out from the metropolis, and on north and south banks brought commuter villas and bungalows to blight the riverside meadows. Mitton's description of Penton Hook graphically illustrates how such places were being rapidly colonized by those who could afford to escape from the crowded city to the countryside.

Penton Hook is quite peculiar. To a select little coterie of people it is *the* place on the river, but to hundreds of others it is not known at all. To its own manifest advantage it is off the 'hard high road', and the scorchers and the bounders, and the multitude generally, fly by within a comparatively short distance, little knowing what they have missed. But one or two of the favoured few turn down to quiet little Laleham, and wheeling round a corner come right on to the tow-path by the river's brink; in a hundred yards they are at Penton Hook. But though the Hook is very select and highly favoured, that is not to say it lacks population, only – it is a population of the right sort. Little camps of charming bungalows dot the banks both above and below the lock. Some are built on ground leased from the

Bell Weir Lock

The Swan Uppers at London Stone, Staines

Staines Bridge

Conservancy, some on that of private owners. To each man is allotted a strip of ground, with so much river frontage, whereon he builds to his own taste and fancy a little one-storeyed white-painted house, and lays out the tiny garden from which his own white steps reach down to the water.

The trees near the bungalows, and those that fringe the meadows near, are not pollarded; there is space between their tall stems. The short grass, gemmed with pink-tipped daisies, can be seen everywhere, and there is air, and freshness, and openness for everyone. The white paint of the bungalows and their neat green or pink roofs, the rows of geraniums, roses, and other flowers carefully kept and tended, add touches of gaiety and brightness.

There are three weirs, for the river here makes the neatest horse-shoe in its whole length, and the authorities have cut through the neck of land, so that the greater part of the stream

Penton Hook Lock

goes rioting and tumbling in joyous confusion beneath the great new weir, provided with a pent-house roof, under which it is always cool on the hottest summer day, with transparent reflections dancing on the wall and a ripple and splash below. The second weir, a mere tumbling-weir, is only a few yards away. The water does not often leap over it unless it is at flood time, when it affords a safety outlet. The third and widest is a mixture, half sluice gates and half of the tumbling kind. At one time there was no weir here, and boats could avoid the lock by navigating the Hook, but that is now no longer possible. There is one advantage in it; it keeps the Hook more secluded. The little red water-gauge house is connected by wires with Staines, and so to all the rest of England. By an automatic arrangement, the register shows simultaneously here and at the offices of the water company what depth of water there is, so that they may know how much they can take.

Laleham Ferry

At Penton it should be always summer, with dog-roses and sweetbriar, with placid red cows grazing on the tender grass, with boats tethered in a lazy current round the bend of the Hook.

An uncommonly good place for fishing it is, this Hook, as the kingfishers have found out, for they are yearly increasing, and apparently do not mind the gay tide of summer company that invades their haunts. Right down on the banks near the lock one pair nested this year. No steamers churn up the waters and frighten the fish; only a slow-moving houseboat or two towed to position and there left, or those drifting boats belonging to young men and maidens who are content to drift metaphorically as well as actually.

The Abbey river starts away on its own account on the far side of the Hook, and begins its short course of about a couple of miles, to fall into the Thames again at Chertsey. It used to be possible to get up it in a boat, but now it is barred. However, visitors have nothing to complain of, for the meadows around are singularly open to them, and the place is not hedged about with restrictions as are so many river resorts. Numbers of people come down to picnic, and it is no uncommon sight to see quite a row of motors outside the lock-keeper's house, while footman or chauffeur carries across the luncheon hampers to what was once a peninsula but is now an island. Tradesmen's carts come round too, finding in the swallow-colony quite enough demand to make it worth their while; and year by year the bungalows grow. A whole new piece of meadow, hitherto osier bed, is even now going to be devoted to them. 'Why, I get as many as twenty to thirty applications for land every week', says the lock-keeper. It is to be hoped Penton Hook will not become over-populated, or the delightful freedom from conventionality which now characterises it might die away. 'Ladies who come down here – why, some of them, they never put a hat on their heads the whole time, and I was going to say not shoes or

Shepperton

stockings either!' The place is particularly sought after by theatrical people. Miss Ellen Terry still holds the bungalow she has had for many years. It is surprising how early the season begins; even at the end of chilly March a few of the first of the swallows appear.

Further down river between Chertsey and Shepperton, Godfrey Turner compares the timeless rural scene to that which was being destroyed elsewhere, and follows later with caustic comments about Victorian litter-louts.

Cattle are feeding on the grass of Chertsey Mead, or cooling themselves in the shallow stream. How different are they from the droves of builders and architects who try to improve the banks of the river! The cattle positively decline all effort at picturesqueness; but they are picturesque, which the new houses or villas, and stuck-up towers and turrets, with all their ornamental pretence, decidedly are not.

Largely frequented by anglers, Weybridge must take care if it desires to retain the favour of boating men. While the towing-path crosses the boat-yard, and dredging is neglected by those, whoever they may be, on whom the duty rests, it is very difficult to avoid grounding; so that many owners have been taking their boats away, as the constant scratching not only scratches but strains them. Shepperton on the Middlesex shore, is a pretty village, small and quiet, with its chief places of residence hidden away behind trees, or peeping out upon the river. It has a railway terminus, on the South-Western system, and is about an hour, that is, nineteen miles, from Waterloo. The deeps afford tolerable fly-fishing in the trout season, and are more frequently fished for jack, perch, roach, and barbel. There are several good swims in pretty equal favour for anglers, to wit the upper deep, the lower deep, and the old deep, east of the creek rails. Besides these, the creek itself is often resorted to. The anglers' inns at Shepperton are the Anchor and the Crown. It is an unspoilt Thames-side village, this Shepperton, in spite of its many pleasure-seeking visitors; a class, to say the sad truth, apt to disclose a selfish indifference to the pleasure of others. If the holiday-maker is to be traced by scientific investigation, the marks to be looked for will be broken bottles, greasy sandwich-papers, and lobster-shell, just as flint tools and weapons denote other and earlier savages who have lived on earth, and have made it as disagreeable as possible for their fellow-brutes. Shepperton Lock and Ferry are both picturesque in themselves, as well as being foregrounds of scenery that is charming to the eye nurtured by art.

The Anglers Inn, Walton

The district from Shepperton to Hampton, being conveniently placed for a day's excursion from London, was a favourite weekend stamping ground for vast numbers of anglers. The extraordinary increase in the popularity of the sport had brought about the implementation of Thames fishery by-laws, such as the establishment of a close season, methods of fishing, and limits on the size and number of fish that could be taken away. John Leyland, describing the district on his way upstream in his THE THAMES ILLUSTRATED, tells us something about the organization of the sport.

Hampton, and Sunbury beyond, may be described as a headquarters of fishing in the middle waters, or lower angling grounds, of the river. Tagg's Island, and other eyots hereabout,

Angling below Sunbury Weir

are famous resorts of anglers. Near Sunbury are special rearing ponds, out of which thousands of young fish are turned into the river every year, and there are excellent deeps where the angling is very good. The Thames Angling Preservation Society is a body which protects the fishery under the Thames Conservancy, and has water-bailiffs and watchers along the river. The wary angler would do well to make himself familiar with the regulations, and with the fence months for trout, jack, roach, dace, barbel, gudgeon, chub, etc., and to remember that the watchers may enter his boat and seize any fish or spawn illegally taken, as well as the instruments used for their capture. The boatman, too, may be advised to ascertain his rights and privileges in regard to picnics and camps on the islands and banks. So will bad blood be spared, and nought trouble digestion or other pleasures of the placid Thames. This is not

the place in which to deal at any length with fishing in the river, but it must be noted that all along the bank there are angling resorts at the various villages, and old hostelries which welcome the votaries of the gentle art.

Sunbury, which they greatly haunt – for trout may be taken by the long rushing weir – lies about two miles beyond Hampton, a pleasant old-fashioned village, straggling along the Middlesex bank, with old redbrick dwellings, fine trees, and much to make it attractive. Its church is a plain and unpretentious structure, but the village, seen from the water through the willows, presents a very pretty picture.

Within a few miles of Kingston, the starting point of the epic voyage of THREE MEN IN A BOAT, we view Molesey Lock through the eyes of Jerome K. Jerome, who supposed it to be the busiest on the river. Regretfully, there is only space for part of his discourse on river dress.

I have stood and watched it sometimes, when you could not see any water at all, but only a brilliant tangle of bright blazers, and gay caps and saucy hats, and many-coloured parasols, and silken rugs, and cloaks, and streaming ribbons, and dainty whites; when looking down into the lock from the quay, you might fancy it was a huge box into which flowers of every hue and shade had been thrown pell-mell, and lay piled up in a rainbow heap, that covered every corner.

On a fine Sunday it presents this appearance nearly all day long, while, up the stream, and down the stream, lie, waiting their turn, outside the gates, long lines of still more boats; and boats are drawing near and passing away, so that the sunny river, from the palace up to Hampton church is dotted and decked with yellow, and blue, and orange, and white, and red, and pink. All the inhabitants of Hampton and Moulsey dress themselves up in a boating costume, and come and mooch

Molesey Lock

round the lock with their dogs, and flirt, and smoke, and watch the boats, and, altogether, what with the caps and jackets of the men, the pretty coloured dresses of the women, the excited dogs, the moving boats, the white sails, the pleasant landscape, and the sparkling water, it is one of the gayest sights I know of near this dull old London town.

The river affords a good opportunity for dress. For once in a way, we men are able to show *our* taste in colours, and I think we come out very natty, if you ask me. I always like a little red in my things – red and black. You know my hair is a sort of golden brown, rather a pretty shade I've been told, and a dark red matches it beautifully; and then I always think a light-blue necktie goes so well with it, and a pair of those Russian-leather shoes and a red silk handkerchief round the waist – a handkerchief looks so much better than a belt.

Harris always keeps to shades or mixtures of orange or yellow

Sunbury waterworks

but I don't think he is at all wise in this. His complexion is too dark for yellow. Yellows don't suit him; there can be no question about it. I want him to take to blue as a background, with white or cream for relief; but, there! the less taste a person has in dress, the more obstinate he always seems to be. It is a great pity because he will never be a success as it is, while there are one or two colours in which he might not really look so bad, with his hat on . . .

Mitton, too, was suitably impressed with Molesey and the surrounding area, and takes us on to bustling Kingston.

Molesey Lock, just above the bridge, is a popular place in summer. All those who have come down to enjoy the fresh air, and who want an excuse for doing nothing, stand and watch the boats passing through; there is always as great a crowd on the tow-path as on the water. A number of islands lie above the lock, the largest of which is Tagg's, as well known as any island on the river, and much patronized by holiday-makers at lunch and tea-time. In summer a band plays on the lawn twice a week. It is opposite the end of the Hurst Park Racecourse, patronized by altogether a different type of people from those who come to Hampton Court, and who can only be said to belong to the river accidentally, by reason of the position of the course. A wonderful club boat-house of polished wood has sprung up of recent years on the Hampton side, and above it is Garrick's Villa with portico and columns. This the great actor bought in 1754 and kept until his death, after which his widow lived in it for another forty years. He was visited here by all the celebrated men of his time, including Horace Walpole, Dr Johnson and Hogarth, and here he gave a splendid series of river fêtes. The little temple on the bank was built by him as a shrine for a statue of Shakespeare, which has now been removed. A small public garden on the edge of the water makes this a favourite lounging place for the people of the neighbourhood. The scenery is rather tame, but has that charm always to be found in flowing water and green grass, in the absence of chimneys and other horrors of man's making.

The church of Hampton village stands up fairly high above the water. It is in a most unlovely style, but ivy has done something to smooth down its defects, which are further toned by distance. There is a ferry close by, and as this is the nearest point to the station, many of those who arrive by train on race days cross at this point, and the ferrymen reap rich harvests.

Not far beyond this loom up the great earthworks and reservoirs of the West Middlesex and Grand Junction Water Company, and with that the influence of Hampton may be said to cease.

The Swan Hotel, Thames Ditton

Returning again to the bridge at Hampton, we have the River Mole flowing in on the right bank. Molesey Regatta takes place every year in July. The trees and red brickwork of the palace are on the left, and only a short way down is the pretty little oasis of Thames Ditton, which somehow seems as if it ought to belong to the river much higher up, and had fallen here by mistake. The Swan Inn is right on the edge of the water. It is proud of the fact that Theodore Hook wrote a verse on a pane of glass at a time when such things were quite legitimate, because the tourist, as we know him had not then come into existence to vulgarize the practice. The pane has been broken, but the verse is remembered, and the following lines are a sample:

> The Swan, snug inn, good fare affords
> As table e'er was put on,

And worthier quite of loftier boards,
Its poultry, fish and mutton.
And while sound wine mine host supplies,
With ale of Meux and Tritton,
Mine hostess with her bright blue eyes
Invites to stay at Ditton.

We wonder how many hostesses since have wished the lines had never been written. An old inn nearby, with overhanging gable end and clinging wistaria, makes a pretty corner, and in the High Street itself there are bits so different from the Kingston and Surbiton ideal, that one cannot understand how they can be in the same zone with them at all. The green lawns of Ditton House and Boyle Farm are quite close and the fine island with its willows hides the flatness of the further bank.

The reach is a favourite one for sailing boats. Below Long Ditton are the large waterworks of the Lambeth Company. On fine Saturdays and Sundays the Hampton tow-path on the other side is generally alive with people. On Raven's Ait is the club house of the Kingston Rowing Club, and beside the water runs a well laid out strip of ground with bushes and seats, and a good stout hedge to keep off the dust from the motor cars which race by on the road – a section of the Ripley road beloved of scorchers. In summer this little public garden is bright with flowers, and it is a great favourite with the inhabitants of

The Thames at Molesey

Kingston and Surbiton. Before arriving at the bridge there are the backs of untidy houses, and generally a great medley of barges, laden with hay and bricks and coal, lying about by the wharves.

CHAPTER FIVE

The Tidal Thames

Two miles below Kingston Bridge the broad reach is barred by the long line of sluice-gates of Teddington Weir, the lowest on the Thames. The weir and its attendant lock were first constructed in timber in 1811, but became ramshackle in a comparatively short time. The lock was rebuilt in stone in 1859 and, because of the growth of pleasure traffic, a small skiff lock was built alongside. The Conservancy rebuilt the weir in 1869, and enlarged it in the 1880s when extensive dredging also took place in the reaches above and below. At the end of the Victorian era the increase in the size and number of commercial barges moving inland from London Docks necessitated the construction of the massive barge lock, opened in 1904. Prior to that, in 1893, the noisome mudflats at low tide below Teddington, complained of by our correspondent, J. Penderel-Brodhurst, had been remedied, or at least the upper portion of them drowned, by the construction of Richmond tide sluices and lock.

Teddington is but a couple of miles, as the river flows, from Kingston, and for the last half mile of the distance the murmur, one might almost say sometimes the roar, of the weir is audible. This same weir is the prime delight of the angler upon the more 'Cockneyfied' portion of the river, and many is the patient piscator who perches himself thereon betimes, and sits at the receipt of finny custom until the gathering dusk renders the enterprise no longer profitable.

Adjoining the weir is the lock, the first in the ascent and the last in the descent of the river. The lock and weir mark, to all

Kingston waterfront

intents and purposes, the spot, between sixty or seventy miles from the sea, at which the Thames ceases to be tidal. Henceforth the pilgrim, following the river on its way to the ocean, will see at low water, particularly between here and Kew Bridge, more mud-banks than he cares to count. At such times, too, the sense of smell will, at all events in hot weather, be

River Wey barges leaving Teddington Lock

hedgerows filled with poppies cease, and a very matter-of-fact embankment on the Surrey shore has to be reckoned with. Yet the reach between the lock and Eel Pie Island has always been popular, and often in the summer one may see here all sorts and conditions of notabilities disporting themselves at a little water-party. We are coming now to classic ground, where wit and letters, fashion and frivolity, long have reigned. There is not another village in England with literary associations so numerous and august as Twickenham. Pope and Walpole are the presiding genii — neither of them, perhaps, the most genial of genii; but the fairy-like element is supplied by the hosts of feminine friends with whom the two bachelors were wont to philander. . .

It is in the neighbourhood of Pope's villa that the injury which has been done to the Thames by the mass of sewage sludge that has been so recklessly poured into it of late years first becomes noticeable. Although the effects of the tide are not much felt above Richmond Bridge, the condition of the river hereabouts at low water is lamentable. A broad edging of slimy ooze stretches for some distance from the bank on either side, and when the weather is really hot, and there is a drought of any considerable duration, as happened in the summer 1884, the odour is hardly that of frankincense. The Thames Conservancy embankment between Twickenham and Richmond will no doubt improve matters somewhat; but it is to say the least, melancholy that it should have become necessary to so disfigure the Surrey shore. Nor does the presence of unwieldy dredges [dredgers] in these reaches enhance the picturesqueness of the stream, while the new towing-path made with dried mud from the river-bed is an agency of martyrdom.

We are now out onto waters ruled by the tides: dangers lurk for those that are not acquainted, or do not respect them; but heed them and they

found to have taken so keen a development that even chloride of lime would be accounted an odour sweeter than that given forth by the nude expanse of festering mud. At Teddington as yet there is happily little annoyance of this kind. To see the little of interest the village affords it is necessary to land at the ferry opposite the Anglers, an old-fashioned inn which has long been popular with fishermen. . . .

From Teddington Lock until close to Richmond the stream is undeniably less picturesque. The river is less full of water, and when the tide is out the unsightly and unsavoury mud-banks are always in view. The towing-path becomes stony and arid; the

Teddington Lock from below

will be of great service. The broad expanse of the tidal Thames was for many centuries a vital western highway from the City and the Port of London, with craft carrying passengers and goods to and fro, under sail or hauled from the towing-path by horses or gangs of men assisted by the run of the tide. In the Victorian Age a great many barges and lighters, under sail or oars, or towed by steam tugs ('mercantile tin kettles', according to William Morris), still made their way up to Brentford Dock and their cargoes transferred onto the canal system, or through Teddington Lock to Kingston and beyond, much to the displeasure of some rowing gentlemen, who thought the river was theirs alone. Although many fine stately houses overlooked the river, the village waterfronts of the tideway were generally of a very work-worn appearance. In 1847 James Thorne in his RAMBLES BY RIVERS. looked with disfavour at Strand-on-the-Green, but elsewhere the view was much to his liking. However, the construction of Barnes Railway Bridge was an ominous sign of change.

Twickenham Ferry

The Collection of irregular dirty-looking houses which border the Thames just below Kew Bridge is Strand-on-the-Green, a hamlet of Chiswick. It chiefly consists of malting houses, barge builders' sheds, and hovels for boatmen, fishermen, and field labourers; but there are a few houses of the better class . . . Though the banks of the Thames between Kew and Chiswick are everywhere low and level, yet they are so diversified by the succession of open meadows, well-wooded plantations, villages, mansions, and glimpses of distant uplands, while the broad stream flows along in such easy windings, that every one who floats along it acknowledges its agreeable character. On an autumnal evening, as the sun is sinking in the west, the row or

sail upon this part of the river is perfectly delicious. A railway bridge is now being constructed over the Thames by Barnes Terrace, which will probably a good deal alter the appearance of the river here; as the embankment has changed the appearance of the common.

Thorne was writing as the river was dying, poisoned by pollution; within a decade came the years of the 'Big Stink'. Sixty years on, after astonishing effort and expenditure the pollution was within acceptable limits, and nearly all was sweetness and light on the upper tideway when G.E. Mitton passed through.

Richmond, like nearly all the other places on the river, has an atmosphere of its own, difficult to put into words. It is less flippant than Kingston, and has not a tinge of the gravity of Twickenham. The houses rise high and are irregular; those in the main street recede from the water as they leave the bridge, and between them and the stream are innumerable others, some with gardens, some overshadowed by trees. Weeping willows, Scotch firs, and ivy-covered trunks abound, and the place is the perfection of a residential quarter. There is enough oldness and irregularity to avoid stiffness, enough modernity to ensure cleanliness. The bridge has a peculiarly individual curve – a real humpback – and its stone balustrade is very fine. At the southern end, far too many new redbrick flats are springing up, alas! but on the north or east, where lies old Richmond, they are not visible to any appreciable extent. The scene below the bridge is distinctly pretty. Large boat-building yards, as at Kingston, occupy the foreground, and the warm cinnamons and ochres of newly varnished boats are generally to be seen, as well as the more crude and garishly painted craft. The islands are tree-covered, and are well placed in the stream. Yet one may note that, popular as Richmond is, it is not flooded in the summer-time with such crowds of boating visitors as Hampton.

Strand-on-the-Green

A view from Richmond Bridge

There are more large craft about, and boating people do not care for that.

Very few people realize what a large basin there is on the river Brent, and what an amount of business is carried on here. From the river, one's chief reflection is thankfulness that the trees on the large islands have grown so well that they form a screen for the soap factories, the cement works, the breweries, etc., which constitute the industries of Brentford.

The dirty streets are still there, with the confusion in their narrow limits worse confounded by the passing of tramcars, which, over the mile along which Brentford spreads itself, take double the time spent on any other bit of equal distance on their route.

All along the Kew side, up to the bridge, are tea-gardens sandwiched between boat-houses; and the new bridge made of granite, with its branching lamps and royal arms, is really an

Low tide at Kew

imposing object. Above and below the bridge the character of the river is singularly different. Above, as we have seen, are the mud-flats, and wharves, and chimneys, not to omit water towers and gasometers; and below is a bit of Chiswick, built along by the waterside, a queer little irregular row of red-brick houses and cottages, near which are fastened the boats of men who live by fishing; it is a little riverside place of the old sort. There are meadows, called Duke's Meadows, opposite Mortlake, these

afford a fine vantage-ground for spectators who come to see the great Boat Race.

The hour of the Boat Race varies according to the tide, for the race is rowed at the 'top of the tide' – when it is at its fullest. If the hour be an easy one – about midday – and the weather is promising, and especially if the reports of the prowess of the crews give reason to believe the race will be a close one, then the crowd is very large indeed. Some prefer to watch

Skiffs for hire at Hammersmith

Putney Bridge on Boat Race Day

the start; some enthusiasts keep up with the boats on water the whole way; but a great majority there are who want to see the last effort between Hammersmith and Barnes bridges, for it is almost a certainty that the crew leading at Barnes Bridge will be the winner. Almost, but not quite; for there was an occasion when, by a sudden spurt, the positions of the boats were reversed, and Cambridge, which had been behind, won the race. The road along by Mortlake is lined with crowds; every window is filled, and all available roofs. On the railway bridge are closely packed ranks of people, brought there and deposited by trains, which afterwards decorously withdraw and wait to pick them up again. The price of this first-rate position is included in the fares. Chiswick meadows afford space for many more persons, who usually pay a shilling a head to the land-holders. This is a very favourite position, because the grassy slopes form such a pleasant seat while the inevitable waiting is gone through.

In the river itself lie several steamers packed with passengers, and also various small boats. Then down comes the launch of the Thames Conservators to clear the course. The long strings of barges, which have been taking advantage of the flowing tide to make their way upstream, are seen no more. A gun goes off, and then, an extraordinarily short time after, a murmur begins among the crowds on the Mortlake side. It grows and grows and swells along the Chiswick shore, as first one boat creeps round the corner, and then the other. 'Cambridge wins; Cambridge, Cambridge!' 'Row up, Oxford!'

Then, perhaps – usually – it is seen that one boat is leading by so many lengths as to make it impossible for the other to catch up. The leading boat goes ahead with a straight, splendid swing into clear water. The losing one, getting into its opponent's wash, rocks as it labours on, its crew lose heart, and the distance widens.

The umpire's launch follows and a dozen others gliding along, keeping just behind the backward crew. And when all have passed, the river, so calm before, is churned up into miniature waves that wash and beat on the banks. Presently the umpire's boat is seen coming swiftly back, bearing the winning flag at the bows over the other.

The trains move slowly forward to pick up the passengers; bicycles, motors, and carriages begin to move off; streams of people pour down every road; and all is over for another year.

At about the same time the naturalist C.J. Cornish described in THE NATURALIST ON THE THAMES the quietly busy, day-to-day tideway. It was clean enough then, before it was fouled again by indifference and two world wars, for commercial fishing to once again be a viable proposition.

It was the end of a blazing hot London day when I went down the hard to the water's edge, among the small, pink-legged boys, paddling, and the usual group of contemplative workmen, who smoke their pipes by the landing-place. The river was half empty, and emptying itself still more as the ebb ran down. The haze of heat and twilight blurred shapes and colours, but the fine old houses of the historic Mall, the tower of the church, and the tall elms and taller chimneys of the breweries, which divide with torpedo boats the credit of being the staple industries of Chiswick, stood out all black against the evening sky; the clashing of the rivetters had ceased in the shipyard, but the river was cheerfully noisy; many eights were practising between the island and the Surrey bank, coaches were shouting at them, a tug was taking a couple of deal-loaded barges to a wood wharf with much puffing and whistling, and bathers, sheltered by the eyot willows, were keeping up loud and breathless conversations. 'Not exactly the kind of surroundings the fishermen seeks,' you will say; but, apparently, London fish get used to noise. Our boat was what I, speaking unprofessionally, should call a small sea-boat, but I believe she was built years ago at Strand-on-the-Green, the pretty old village with maltings and poplar trees that fringes the river below Kew Bridge. She was painted black and red, and furnished with a shelf, rimmed with an inch-high moulding inboard and drained by holes, to catch the drip from the net as it was hauled in. We were at work in two minutes. The net was fastened at one end to two buoys; these dropped down with the ebb, and formed a fixed, yet floating, point – if that is not a bull – from which the boat was rowed in a circle while one of the brothers who own the boat payed out the net. Thus we kept rowing in circles, alternately dropping and hauling in the net, as we slipped down what was once the Bishop of London's Fishery towards Fulham. There are still no flounders on the famous Bishop's Muds, but other fish were in evidence at once. Though the heat had made them go to the bottom, we had one or two at every haul. The two fishermen were fine specimens of strong, well-built Englishmen. The pace at which they hauled in the net, or rowed the boat round, was great; the rower could complete the circle – a wide one – in a minute, and the net was hauled in in less time, if the hauler chose to. Dace were our main catch – bright silvery fish, about three to the pound, for they do not run large in the tideway; but they were in perfect condition, and quite as good to eat, when cooked, as fresh herring. For some reason the Jews of London prefer these fresh-water fish; they eat them, not as the old Catholics did, on fasts, but for feasts. They will fetch 2d. each at the times of the Jews' holidays, so our fisherman told me, and find a ready sale at all times, though at low prices. Formerly the singularly bright scales were saved to make mother-of-pearl, or rather, to coat objects which were wished to resemble mother-of-pearl. After each haul the fish were dropped into a well in the middle of the boat. A few roach were taken, and an eel; but the most interesting part of the catch was the smelts. These sea-fish now ascend the Thames as they did before the river was polluted. We took about a dozen, some of very large size; they smelt exactly like freshly sliced cucumber. I stayed for an hour, till the twilight was turning to dark, and the tugs' lights began to show. We had by then caught seventy fish, or rather more than one per minute; a hundred is a fair catch on a summer evening. In winter very large hauls are made; then the fish congregate in holes and corners. In summer they are all over the river. When the net happens to enclose one of these shelter holes, hundreds may be taken. Consequently the two fishermen work regularly all through the winter. Sometimes their net is like iron wire, frozen into stiff squares.

In 1885, on the way to Putney and Fulham, Professor T.G. Bonney described in THE ROYAL RIVER what was then the last

Old Putney Bridge

stretch of river before London where green fields and marshes could still be seen. There was also room enough on the river for the sport of rowing, which mainly took place during evenings and weekends and did not clash with commercial traffic. That year the impressive new Putney Bridge was almost complete, replacing an incredible timber structure which had been unsafe for many years but which had been a favourite subject for artists.

The reach of the river from Hammersmith to Putney is comparatively quiet, and the marshy condition of the left bank has compelled the builder to keep at a distance; so that though lines of houses may be seen inland, they are parted from the water by extensive osier beds. We turn our backs disgustedly on the cement works, and glance forward to the more open country beyond, where are houses scantily scattered among trees, and the Old Crab Tree inn. On the right bank a considerable tract of meadow-land still remains unenclosed, on which occasionally there is some fair hedgerow timber, and from which, in summer, the pleasant scent of new-mown grass is wafted; willows rustle by the towing-path, and the white poplar sheds its downy seeds beneath our feet. Bushes grow freely on the river bank, and now and then, for a moment, hide the water. For the last time, if no snorting steamer or screaming steam launch, laden with holiday-makers, chance to be in sight, or, still worse, in hearing, the Thames resumes something of its former peaceful aspect, although the fact that the tidal character of the river has now become conspicuous makes it needful to consult the almanack before paying it a visit – at least, for those who desire to appreciate the real beauty of the scene. . . .

Barn Elms passed, we approach the twin villages – though the term is no longer applicable, for they are now suburbs of London – of Putney and of Fulham, one on either side of the stream. Much alike in their churches, they still differ in other characteristics. For many years Putney has been a centre of London aquatics, which have set their mark on the riverside. Except for the broader stream, our Oxonian or Cantab might fancy himself at certain spots by Cam or Isis. There are the boat-houses of the same nondescript pattern, the sheds sheltering eights and fours and 'funnies' – or whatever name be used to designate the cranky one-man racing boats – the usual flags indicating the headquarters of the different rowing clubs, the usual specimens of the amphibious race that is peculiar to the riverside where oarsmen most do congregate; in short, the waterside at Putney is a rather odd, not wholly unpicturesque, and somewhat unique bit of Thames scenery.

From Putney onwards the Thames truly belonged to the City and its commerce. Mr and Mrs Hall in 1859 viewed the Surrey bank with much alarm.

Battersea Pier and paddle-steamers

There is but a succession of factories and small cottage houses, which serve to shelter labourers and artizans; unwholesome-looking swamps divide the space with yards, and quays, and wagon-sheds, auxiliaries to manufactories of gin, soap, starch, silk, paper, candles, beer, and vitriol.

The effluent from all such manufacturing processes went straight into the river.

Forward in time again to 1885 when Edmund Ollier in THE ROYAL RIVER *found the alleys of Battersea more quaint than alarming. But did he live long enough to be alarmed by Battersea Power Station and its like? The year 1885 also saw the dismantling of the decrepit timber bridge between Battersea and Chelsea; it had been similar in appearance to Old Putney Bridge. The new Battersea Bridge opened in 1890.*

It is at Battersea and Chelsea that the Thames first acquires unmistakably the character of a metropolitan stream. Hamlets there are, higher up, which announce the proximity of a great capital; but here is the capital itself, though only the rudimentary beginnings, or to speak more correctly, the scattered ends. Looking down the channel from this point of view, we see on both sides abundant evidence of crowded life – of industry on the river – the penny steamboat, plies to and fro on its frequent errands. On shore, the vehicles of London bring something of its noise. Yet there is plenty of quiet in both these old-fashioned suburbs; and, although innovation has been at work here as elsewhere, nooks may be found, both in Battersea and Chelsea, which have all the character of a sleepy old country town. Battersea, in particular, is the most straggling oddity in the neighbourhood of London – a grave, slow, otiose place, lulled with the lapping of waves, soothed with the murmur of trees in unsuspected gardens, troubled but little with the clamour of passing trains, and dreaming, perhaps, of eighteenth-century days, when there were mansions in the land, and my Lord Bolingbroke had his family seat near the church. The river here makes a somewhat abrupt curve, and gives a dubious outline to the whole locality. Small inlets run up between old walls, dark with the sludge of many years; and the streets and buildings have had to accommodate themselves to the caprices of the stream. Hence it is that, when walking about Battersea, you speedily lose your bearings, and, after following a devious lane which you suppose to be parallel with the river, suddenly find yourself on a bit of shingly strand, with a barge on the limits of the tide, and a general appearance as if the end of all things had been reached.

Battersea, then, is a 'nook-shotten' a place as is the 'isle of Albion' itself, according to Shakespeare. Gardens as old as the time of Queen Anne hide coyly behind walls that permit only

Chelsea from the Battersea shore

the tops of the trees to be discerned. Houses, of the sedate red-and-brown brick that our ancestors loved, stand at oblique angles to the roadways, each with the silent history of vanished generations entombed beneath its ponderous, red-tiled roof. Ancient taverns or inns (call them not public houses, still less hotels or gin palaces) – goodly hostelries of the past, broad-frontaged, deep-windowed, large-chimneyed, many-gabled – invite the most temperate passer-by to refresh himself in the cavernous gloom of the bar. The old parish church – not so old as one could wish, but having a Georgian character that is beginning to acquire the interest of all departed modes – occupies a sort of peninsula on the river, the ripple of which speaks closely in the ears of dead parishioners. On the whole,

Battersea has known better days. It is now chiefly given up to factories, to the humble dwellings of factory people, and to the houses and shops of the lower middle class. But, in the National Society's Training College, it has a noble old mansion, standing in well-timbered grounds; and the free school of Sir Walter St. John (grandfather of Queen Anne's famous minister) is also interesting. The school was founded in 1700, but the building is of the modern Tudor style. To a casual visitor, however, the most noticeable thing about the suburb is the river itself, with its belongings: the straggling banks, the rickety water-side structures, the boat-builders' yards, the heavy, black barges hauled on to the foreshore, undergoing repair, or being lazily broken up, the larger vessels, with sails of that rusty orange hue which tells of sun and breeze, and the prevalent smell of pitch, mingled with watery ooze.

Chelsea is becoming fashionable along the river frontage; but, although the stately red-brick mansions recently erected on the embankment are sumptuous and noble, the chief interest of the locality is in the older parts. The fine old house at the corner of Beaufort Street is an excellent specimen of the kind of suburban dwelling our forefathers used to build, when, the land being far less valuable than now, they spread out broadly and roomily, and were not constrained to pile storey upon storey, until the roofs seem desirous of making acquaintance with the clouds. It is at this point that the Chelsea Embankment commences – a splendid promenade between avenues of plane trees, which every season will make more umbrageous. Several years ago, before the late Sir Joseph Bazalgette began to reclaim the river bank, there was no more picturesque spot in Chelsea, of the dirty, out-at-elbows order, than the bit extending eastward from Battersea Bridge to the old church. Its fantastic irregularity of roof and gable, its dormer windows, its beetling chimney-stacks, its red and brown, its look of somnolent old age and grave

The Victoria Embankment

experience, had something of a Dutch character; but it was certainly not Dutch in point of cleanliness. Picturesque it is still; but the Embankment has swept away that side of the street which was towards the river, while the ragged tenements on the other side await the hands of the destroyer . . .

It is on quitting Westminster Bridge that the Victoria Embankment begins – a magnificent work, containing the finest effects of architecture, mingled with trees and shrubbery, that are to be found in the metropolis. When one recollects the unslightly mud-banks that used to stretch along the shores of the Thames in this part of its course – the grim, dilapidated buildings that approached the water's edge, the general appearance of ruin, the shiftless, disreputable air of the whole locality, save where some great building, such as Somerset House, broke the dull uniformity of dirt, decay, and neglect – it is impossible to be too grateful for what we now possess. The massive river-wall, with the bronze heads of lions starting out of every pier, the extended line of parapet, the artistic lamps reflected at night in the shining stream, the Cleopatra's Needle, with sphinxes round its base, the avenues of planes, the green and leafy gardens, the elevated terrace of the Adelphi, the stately river-front of Somerset House, and the splendid new buildings which have been erected at various points of the route, make up, together with the broad and flowing river, a picture which it would not be easy to surpass. At Charing Cross, unfortunately, there is an irremediable contradiction to this grandeur. The railway bridge which there crosses the Thames is one of the ugliest of an ugly family; and all we can do is to comfort ourselves with a sense of the convenience afforded by such structures, and with the impression of Titanic power always accompanying the transit of vast bodies through the air above our heads. As soon as our backs are turned upon the viaduct, it is forgotten, and close by, at the bottom of Buckingham Street, we come upon a decaying relic of old London, which is worth going to see. The Water Gate, formerly belonging to York House, and built by Inigo Jones for George Villiers, Duke of Buckingham, still outlasts, in melancholy isolation, all the princely splendours that once distinguished this spot.

London's Victorian river frontage, so cruelly treated in the twentieth century by friend and foe alike, represented the working face of one of the world's greatest maritime trading cities, with a chequered history stretching back for two thousand years. The commercial look of the frontage was occasionally relieved by impressive buildings such as Somerset House, Custom House, Billingsgate and the Tower of

St Paul's Cathedral

London, and, rising behind, the spires of Sir Christopher Wren's churches and the magnificent dome of St Paul's Cathedral. Otherwise, wharves and quays, some with names first recorded over a thousand years before, clustered at the river's edge, the row broken only by the approaches to several bridges, including the then recently replaced London Bridge, and narrow alleys leading to ancient river stairs.

English travel writers tried to emphasize the best features of the river but for a down-to-earth and unprejudiced view, we turn to the American novelist Henry James, who took a boat ride down to

Greenwich in 1877. In ENGLISH HOURS he portrays a bleak, work-worn face of London River, the often ugly, dangerous river of the novels of Charles Dickens, but nevertheless, James admits to being impressed.

I find an irresistible charm in any sort of river-navigation, but I scarce know how to speak of the little voyage from Westminster Bridge to Greenwich. It is in truth the most prosaic possible form of being afloat, and to be recommended rather to the inquiring than to the fastidious mind. It initiates you into the duskiness, the blackness, the crowdedness, the intensely commercial character of London. Few European cities have a finer river than the Thames, but none certainly has expended more ingenuity in producing a sordid river-front. For miles and miles you see nothing but the sooty backs of warehouses, or perhaps they are the sooty faces: in buildings so utterly expressionless it is impossible to distinguish. They stand massed together on the banks of the wide turbid stream, which is fortunately of too opaque a quality to reflect the dismal image. A damp-looking, dirty blackness is the universal tone. The river is almost black, and is covered with black barges; above the black housetops, from among the far-stretching docks and basins, rises a dusky wilderness of masts. The little puffing steamer is dingy and gritty – it belches a sable cloud that keeps you company as you go. In this carboniferous shower your companions, who belong chiefly, indeed, to the classes bereft of lustre, assume an harmonious grayness; and the whole picture, glazed over with the glutinous London mist, becomes a masterly composition. But it is very impressive in spite of its want of lightness and brightness, and though it is ugly it is anything but trivial. Like so many of the aspects of English civilization that are untouched by elegance or grace, it has the merit of expressing something very serious. Viewed in this intellectual

Fishing craft at Billingsgate

light the polluted river, the sprawling barges, the dead-faced warehouses, the frowsy people, the atmosphere impurities become richly suggestive. It sounds rather absurd, but all this smudgy detail may remind you of nothing less than the wealth and power of the British Empire at large; so that a kind of metaphysical magnificence hovers over the scene, and supplies what may be literally wanting. I don't exactly understand the association, but I know that when I look off to the left at the East India Docks, or pass under the dark hugely piled bridges, where the railway trains and the human processions are for ever moving, I feel a kind of imaginative thrill. The tremendous piers of the bridges, in especial, seem the very pillars of the Empire aforesaid.

Nearly twenty years later Aaron Watson stood on London Bridge and, like other writers before him, tried to impart the drama of the panorama of crowded shipping lying in the Upper and Lower Pool. In THE ROYAL RIVER *he then takes the reader on towards the estuary, past places associated for centuries with England's maritime heritage: Wapping, Limehouse, Greenwich and Woolwich, and, as the low shoreline imperceptibly widens to meet the sea, Gravesend and Sheerness.*

The crowded shipping of the Pool, the steamers coming and going, the vessels lying at anchor here and there, as if the river were a huge dock, only feebly represent the vast tonnage which is borne on our grand and historic river every day of every year. Behind the great piles of warehouses – towering over the housetops, ornamenting the sky with a curious fretwork of masts and spars and cordage – lie scores and hundreds of vessels of all nations, crowded into dock beyond dock, making a line of rigging, of glittering yards and masts, of furled sails and flaunting canvas, on either side of the Thames for mile on mile.

It is on the Tower side that the line is least broken. London Bridge is scarcely left behind ere St Katharine's and London Docks come in sight; then following the enormous acreage of the East and West India Docks, then come the docks at Millwall, and the Albert and Victoria Docks, stretching onward to North Woolwich – a vast contiguity of dock property, basin beyond basin occupied by some of the finest shipping that roams the seas.

Earlier in the century, when the screw-steamer was as yet undreamed of, and there had been no vision of the steam-tug which is so vast a convenience today, this portion of the river

The Tower of London

presented at certain seasons a much more stirring sight than now. Fleets of vessels, with their sails spread, came in at every tide; hundreds of ships lay crowding in the Thames at the mercy of the wind; it was a long panorama of seafaring life, with no bellying smoke to impede the view. All that has been changed by the wand of Science and the genius of Discovery. If a vessel lies in the stream instead of in the docks, it is for purposes peculiarly its own; and the dock gates, instead of opening to whole fleets driven up by a prosperous wind, wing open to solitary, but more gigantic, vessels propelled by steam.

Not that sailing-ships are no longer numerous in the Thames!

Greenwich Pier

Thames, there is a great lumber of smaller craft, inconvenient but full of interest, greatly in the way, but very delightful to the artist and the heedful possessor of a 'quiet eye'.

No effective justice has ever yet been done to the lower portion of the Thames. You will find it stated in most books on the subject that the river ceases to be picturesque when it has passed St Paul's. A French poet calls it 'an infected sea, rolling its black waters in sinuous detours'; and that is the despondent view that has been taken by the majority of English writers. Yet in the eyes of those who have roamed about this section of the river, and have loved it, only at London Bridge does the Thames become really interesting. In the higher reaches it is an idyllic river, swooning along through pleasant landscapes; after St Paul's it takes on a new and more sombre sort of glory, assumes a mightier interest, and is infinitely more majestic in the lifting of its waters. Above London Bridge, even when the wind is blowing, the waves are small and broken, like those of a mountain lake; in the Pool the water surges and heaves in broad masses, the light seems to deal with it more nobly, and the Thames assumes such majesty as becomes a stream which flows through the grandest city, and bears so great a portion of the commerce of the world.

As for picturesqueness, one may behold a score of the finest possible pictures from London Bridge itself. The grey tower of St Magnus Church, smitten by a passing ray of sunlight, stands out bright and shining behind the dark mass of buildings over Freshwater Wharf; beyond it, more dimly seen, the Monument lifts its flaming crown; the Pool is alive with hurrying steamers and clustering sails; Billingsgate is in the midst of its traffic; the white face of the Custom House looks down into the dun waters; and yonder rise the more sombre walls of our most ancient fortress, the venerable quadragon of the White Tower, with its four dark cupolas, dominating them all.

The old East Indiaman has departed, the ships of John Company are broken to pieces, but the tall three-master is by no means an unfamiliar object, and on the Thames waters below London Bridge one may encounter schooners and brigs and brigantines galore. Nor has the number of lighters and wherries and dumb-barges diminished. When the docks were made, the watermen rose up in revolt against a threatened invasion of their privileges, and were fortunate enough to secure for themselves new rights which ensured their continuance and prosperity. So it happens that in addition to the sailing-ships and schooners which may be seen at anchor along either side of the

Off Tilbury

The front of Billingsgate has altered its aspect of late. A wharf has arisen where, heretofore, a couple of narrow gangways descended sheer to the fore-shore of the Thames, when it was exposed, and to the water, when the tide was in. Many a Billingsgate porter has lost his life hurrying up those gangways, yet, so conservative is the City of London in its habits, that it is only a few years since the conclusion was reached that the market would be no worse, and human life would be all the safer, for a pier. With that very modern improvement one of our London 'sights' has changed its aspect. No longer may we behold the four lines of white-jacketed figures, two bustling up from and two hurrying down to the boats. Yet the white-jacketed figures are there, and they bustle about as of old, though the work has become indescribably easier, and is carried on by men in less constant peril of their lives.

To see Billingsgate in the full tide of its work – and England has no other sight to compare with it – one must rise with the sun in summer, and long before the dawn in winter, when heavily laden market-carts from Kent are rumbling over London Bridge, whilst the mists cling to the surface of the river so heavily as to seem beyond the power of any mere London sunshine to raise or dispel.

At five in the morning, summer or winter, rain or shine, Billingsgate seems to shake itself and start on a sudden into active and turbulent life. In the night a series of long, low, snake-like steamers have crept up the river, bearing freight from the fishing-smacks which are pursuing their dangerous fortune in the North Sea. Just below where they have dropped anchor cluster several broad-beamed, highly polished, Dutch schuyts, bringing oysters or eels to market, and reminding you, by their bulk and build, of the stout, prosperous, slow-moving citizens of Amsterdam. Little panting steam-tugs are hurrying here and there, and amid a confused glare of lights, a tempest of smoke and steam, the Billingsgate porters, having waited for the five o'clock bell, rush out in streams to shuyt and smack and steamer, pushing, shouting, swearing, surging to and fro in the mist and steam and glare, working with the energy of gnomes doomed to perform an allotted task ere the first beams of morning surprise them at their toil.

Thames Street, and Fish Street Hill, and Pudding Lane, and many a street and alley roundabout, are crowded, packed, jammed, with vans and carts and trollies. The stranger wanders bewildered and afraid among all these, in danger of being knocked down by laden porters, run over by market-carts, hustled out of all self-possession by feverish buyers, or lost amongst such a wild and interminable confusion of vehicles as no other place in the world can show. . . .

The beautiful stretches of the Upper River must always offer an attraction to men who have an eye for colour, and to whom the curious spectacle of cultured wildness is pleasant.

But there are some who, while they remember the long reaches where the willow herbs shine and the glassy river rolls, think kindly of the other reaches where the signs of toil begin, and where the great stream pours on between banks that have nothing to redeem them save strangeness of form and infinite varieties of bizarre tints.

A voyage in a small boat from the hill where the Greenwich Observatory cuts sharp against the sky, down to the rushing channels where the black flood flows past the Woolwich Piers, is always unpleasant to those whose senses are delicate, but as soon as we reach Gravesend we come to another region, and there those who care little for brilliance of colour, those who care little for softness of effect, those who care only for stern suggestion, find themselves at home.

One of the pleasantest experiences in life is to wake in the early dawn, put sail on a fast yacht, and run on the tide from Gravesend, past the grim end of the Lower Hope. The colliers weigh anchor, the apple-bowed brigs curtsy slowly on the long rush of swelling water, and as you look up from your cabin you receive sudden and poignant suggestions that tell of far-off regions, and that take you away from the grim world that you have just left behind.

Here is a clumsy black brig bustling the water before her! The ripples fly in creamy rings from her bows; her black topsails, with their queer patches, flap a little as the wind comes and goes, and you hear the hoarse orders given by the man who stands near the helm, and who is in authority for the time. Then a great four-master spreads her wings, and while the little

London River

tug puffs and frets around her as though there were important business to do, which did not allow of a moment's consideration, the big ship slowly slides away, and gathering power under her canvas surges into the brown deep, and takes the melancholy emigrants away towards the Nore.

Then the 'tramps' of the ocean – the ugly colliers – are not without interest. One of them foams up to you, and you know that the man in command of her has perhaps not slept for seventy-two hours. He has made his wallowing rush from the North Country; he has risked all the dangers of fog and darkness and storm, and he has brought his vessel up to the derrick with satisfaction. Then in a few hours the swarm of 'whippers' have cleared her; the rattle of the great cranes has rung through the night, and the vessel has been emptied in a time that would seem astonishing to those who manage sanitary corporation business on shore, and who condemn us to endure the presence of ghastly stenches and unspeakable sights for hour after hour. The anchors are whipped up and the ocean 'tramp' tears away on her trip to the Tyne.

There is not a single sight or sound that does not convey its own interest. If it is autumn time, the racing yachts are clearing for action, dapper men are bounding hither and thither, as though there were nothing in life to be cared for excepting success in the race that must shortly be begun. The gun fires and the lazy breeze of the morning strikes the huge spinnakers, while the razor-bowed craft move slowly out, and gradually gather speed until the troubled water foams in crisp whirls and rolls away aft in long creamy trails.

The upper reaches of the river are lightsome, and given over wholly to pleasure. Every turn conveys the sensation of wealth and comfort; every delicate shallop that floats luxuriously past the locks hints of money acquired in the crush of the great city; but in the Lower River any day the story of stress, and struggle, and coarse labour may be read on the spot, and perhaps nowhere in the world – not even in the huge docks of Liverpool – can so vivid an idea be gained of the mercantile greatness of England. No attempt is made to disguise the natural ugliness and coarseness of every feature in the scene; steamers surge up at half speed, and the vast waves that they throw curl against the bank and bring away masses of mud; the barges glide lazily, the black shrimpers troop down the current with their ragged sails, and everything speaks of a life given over wholly to rough toil.

It is true that many parties come from the City in steamboats, and in the summer evenings the air is full of music, and shrill sounds of laughter ring from the splashing boats as they pass you; but these are only stray visitations, and no one who knows the Lower River, no one who has felt the sentiment of the locality keenly, can ever associate it with light-heartedness. . . .

Thames spritsail barge off Gravesend, carrying hay for London's carriage horses

There is, from some points of view, no more interesting spot on the Thames than Gravesend Reach. Here, after narrowing for a portion of its distance, the river spreads out again, and proceeds on a perfectly straight course to Cliff Creek. Gravesend Reach is three miles and a half in length, and is usually more populous with shipping than any other point between the Nore Light Ship and the Pool. All outward bound ships must take their pilots on board at Gravesend, and so it frequently occurs that here the last farewells are said and the last kisses are given. In the Reach, vessels wait for the changing of the tide, so that at one period of the day it is full of ships with their sails furled, and, at another, of vessels newly spreading their canvas to the wind. A breezy, stirring place is Gravesend Reach, enthralling at all hours and in all weathers, stormy sometimes, sometimes as calm as a lake on a windless night, but most beautiful on grey, uncertain days, when the light shivers downward through flying clouds, and breaks and sparkles on tumbling crests of wave; when the ships at anchor sway hither and thither on the turbulent waters, and make with their masts and cordage a continuous and confused movement against the sky; when the barges coming up from the Medway tear and strain under their canvas like horses impatient of the bit; when the half-furled sail flaps and battles in the wind, and the sea-birds, now darting to the water, now leaping towards the flying clouds, seem to be driven about against their will.

The Thames sailing barges that Aaron Watson mentions, and which Henry Taunt found so photogenic, were at that time approaching their maximum number of over two thousand vessels. They were the work-horses of London River and the Medway, also trading along the south and east coasts; the largest of them crossing the English Channel and Irish Sea. They had evolved over centuries into highly efficient sailing vessels that could be worked by a crew of only two or three. A great variety of cargoes was carried, including hay, manure, bricks, cement, timber, gunpowder, grain and London refuse. In the 1860s, Henry Dodd, who made a fortune from refuse, promoted improvements to barge design and sailing techniques by sponsoring sailing matches. This tradition continues with a number of annual races in which some of the few surviving barges, now all converted to pleasure cruising, compete in friendly rivalry to keep the old skills alive.

No informed Victorian description of Thames barges has been found, therefore, to indulge the present compiler, the year 1930 is turned to for the expert opinion of visiting coasting sailor Edmund Eglinton, crewing on one of the last West Country merchant schooners. He writes in THE LAST OF THE SAILING COASTERS.

The Thames sailing barges when loaded appeared to us to be nearly awash. Some loaded with hay stacked so high that the

huge loose-footed mainsail had to be brailed up otherwise it would have fouled the bales of hay. But they had enormous square-headed topsails set over the sprit, and their staysails in some cases were so low on the foredeck we imagined the helmsman could never see any craft that may be approaching under their lee bow. Then their bowsprits, very slender and long, were bowsed down with the bobstays, in some, so much that they seemed to be pointing down towards the water – like enormous spears. Each of these bowsprits carried one huge jib

Southend-on-Sea

A brig under full sail in the Thames Estuary

set on a stay attached to the topmast head; the pulling power of those jibs must have been immense, each, I should imagine, equal to a pair of mighty shire horses! Captain Cocks had been trading to the London river for years; he would not take any chances with the barges. If we were on opposite tacks and the barge was on the port tack (when two sailing vessels are meeting on opposite tacks, the law of the sea is that the ship on the port tack shall always give way to the other) Captain Cocks would

always take avoiding action in plenty of time. He reasoned that with the huge stacks of timber and bales of hay piled high above the hatchways carried by some of the barges, coupled with the fact that the foot of the staysail on some was so near to the foredeck thus limiting the view of the crew, and usually there were only two men aboard, there was always the risk of their not seeing the other vessel in time.

One would see a man run up a ladder, run forward over the

hay bales, or timber, then down another ladder to the fore deck to attend to his duties. Often the men would have straps around their legs just below the knees, and red handkerchiefs around their necks – like the navvies who used to work for my father on the sea walls at home in the West Country – and this may have had some psychological effect, leading strangers to doubt their nautical ability.

Yes, that morning thrashing to windward in the *Two Sisters* towards Sheerness one had to agree with the captain's caution with regard to the sailing barges. It looked to be dangerous – especially the spear-like bowsprits. Later however I came to know that those fears were groundless. Those barge masters were able and clever mariners, their skills acquired over many generations; their's was a special kind of seafaring, like the trowmen of the River Severn only more so.

Now to end this compiled description of the Victorian Thames we turn from a comparatively recent author to our earliest contributor – W.G. Fearnside and his THAMES AND MEDWAY.

As we enter Sea-Reach, the last of those broad expanses of water for which the Thames is celebrated, Leigh church and village appear, pleasantly situated on the Essex banks. Between Leigh and Southend is placed the city stone; the jurisdiction of the lord mayor of London terminating at this spot. A short distance in advance is Southend, which, previous to the modern attraction of Gravesend, was much frequented in summer, as a bathing-place; and the woody character of the adjacent country, the vast breadth of the river, with its moving scenery and the mouth of the Medway, form a bright and interesting break on the Kentish shore, and create for the spot much picturesque beauty. A terrace, erected on some rising ground, called New Southend, has an elegant appearance from the water. Some distance below this town the beacon, called the 'Nore-Light', is placed, being an immense lamp, fixed in the hulk of a Dutch-built vessel, moored nearly in the centre of the Nore, between what is termed Shoebury Ness and the Isle of Sheppey, in order that vessels should know the bearing of the different shoals, which render the navigation dangerous at the entrance of the Thames. The breadth between the western extremity of the Isle of Grain and Shoebury Ness may be denominated the mouth of the river, and is six miles in extent. At this point the majestic Thames, having preserved that air of placid dignity and imposing grandeur which distinguish so eminently this monarch of British rivers, blends its immense volume of waters with those of the Medway, losing designation and destination, is engulfed in the mighty depths of the ocean.

Sources and Acknowledgements

(Place of publication given only if outside London.)

AUTHORS QUOTED IN THE TEXT

Bonney, T.G., *The Royal River*. Cassell and Co., 1885

Church, A.J., *Isis and Thamesis*. Seeley and Co., 1886

Cornish C.J., *The Naturalist on the Thames*. Seeley and Co., 1902

Dickens, Charles, Jnr., *Dictionary of the Thames*. Dickens, 1880

Eglinton, Edmund, *The Last of the Sailing Coasters*. National Maritime Museum, 1982

Fearnside, W.G., *Tombleson's Thames and Medway*. Black and Armstrong, 1834

Hall, Mr and Mrs S.C., *The Book of the Thames*. Coulsdon, Virtue and Co., 1859

Harper, C.G., *Thames Valley Villages*. Chapman and Hall, 1910

James, Henry, *English Hours*. 1905

Jerome, Jerome K., *Three Men in a Boat*. Bristol, J.W. Arrowsmith, 1889

Leslie, George D., *Our River*. Bradbury, Agnew and Co., 1881

Leyland, John., *The Thames Illustrated*. Geo. Newnes, 1897

Mitton, G.E., *The Thames*. A. and C. Black, 1906

Ollier, E., *The Royal River*

Penderel-Brodhurst, J., *The Royal River*

Pennell, Joseph and Elizabeth, *The Stream of Pleasure*. T. Fisher Unwin, 1891

Robertson, H.R., *Life on the Upper Thames*. Virtue, Spalding and Co., 1875

Senior, W,. *The Royal River*

Taunt, Henry, *A New Map of the River Thames*. Oxford, Taunt and Co., 1871

Thorne, James, *Rambles by Rivers. The Thames*. C. Cox, 1847

Turner, G.W., *The Royal River*

Vincent, J.E., *The Story of The Thames*. Smith, Elder and Co., 1909

Watson, A., *The Royal River*

Williams, Alfred, *Round About the Upper Thames*. Duckworth and Co., 1922

OTHER WORKS CONSULTED

Armstrong, W., *The Thames from its rise to the Nore*. Coulsdon, Virtue and Co., 1889

Bolland, R., *Victorians on the Thames*. Midas Books, 1974

Burstall, Patricia, *The Golden Age of the Thames*. Newton Abbot, David and Charles, 1981

Byrne, L. and Churchill, E., *The Eton Book of the River*. Spottiswoode, Ballantyne and Co., 1935

Cleaver, H., *A History of Rowing*. Herbert Jenkins, 1957

Cooke, C.H., *Thames Rights and Wrongs*. Constable and Co., 1895

Dix, F.L., *Royal River Highway*. Newton Abbot, David and Charles, 1985

Gunther, R.T., *The Oxford Country*. John Murray, 1922

Henderson, P,. *William Morris*. Thames and Hudson, 1967

Linney, A.G., *The Lure and Lore of London River*. Sampson Low, Marston and Co., 1930

Phillips, G., *Thames Crossings*. Newton Abbot, David and Charles, 1981

Salter, John H., *Salter's Guide to the Thames*. 1st edn., *c.* 1881

Thacker, F.S., *The Stripling Thames*. Thacker, 1909

——, *The Thames Highway*
    vol. 1 *General History*. Thacker, 1914
    vol. 2 *Locks and Weirs*. Thacker, 1920

Thames Conservancy, *Centenary Handbook*, 1957

'W.H.R.', *The Rowing Almanack and Oarsman's Companion*. Kent and Co., 1862

ACKNOWLEDGEMENTS

The extract from *The Last of the Sailing Coasters* by Edmund Eglinton is reproduced by kind permission of the National Maritime Museum and HMSO. The author is grateful to The Oxfordshire Photographic Archive, at The Centre for Oxfordshire Studies, for use of the photographs.

Index

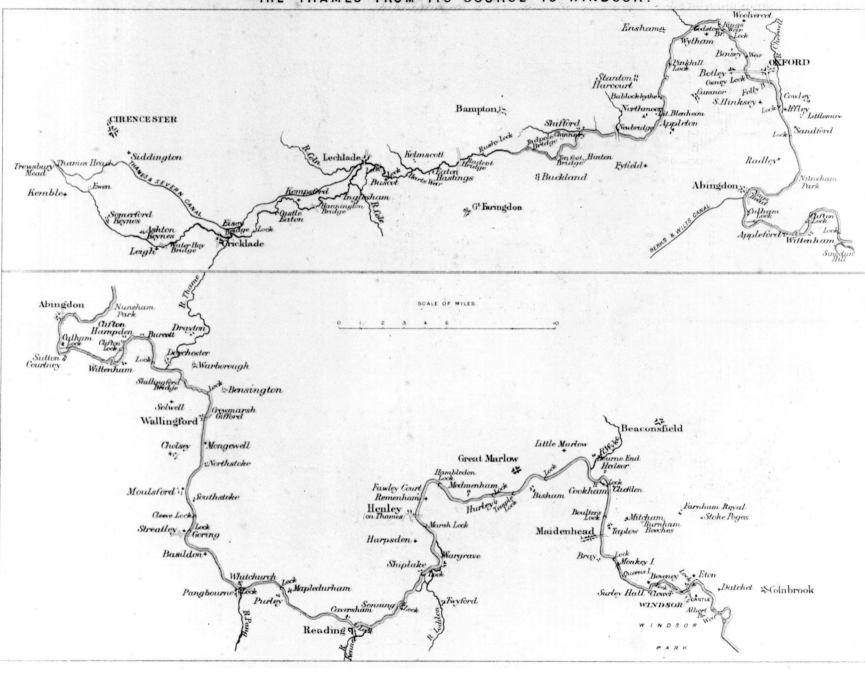

THE THAMES FROM ITS SOURCE TO WINDSOR.